Instrument of

Alan Paton was born in 1903 in Pietermaritzburg, Natal. After attending Pietermaritzburg College, he went on to Natal University, graduating with a degree in Maths and Physics and a Dip. Ed. From 1933–1948 he was Principal of Diepkloof Reformatory (Transvaal) for 700 delinquent African boys. Here he introduced reforms that were to transform a grim prison-like institution into a school. He was appointed Honorary Commissioner of Toc H in South Africa after the death of his friend Jan Hofmeyr, and worked at their tuberculosis settlement in Natal until 1953, when he left to devote his energies to the newly formed Liberal Party.

In 1960, on his return from receiving the Freedom House Award in New York, his passport was confiscated. In 1968 the Liberal Party, of which he was President, was outlawed by the South African Government's Prohibition of Political Interference Bill. He has two sons and lives in Natal.

Mr. Paton's other books include *Cry, the Beloved Country*, *Too Late the Philarope*, *South Africa and Her People*, *Debbie Go Home* (short stories), *Hofmeyr* (biography), and *Kontakion For You Departed*, an autobiographical tribute to his wife who died in 1967.

ACKNOWLEDGMENTS

Grateful acknowledgment is made to the following publishers and authors for permission to use copyrighted material from the titles listed:

Coward-McCann, Inc., New York—Elizabeth Goudge, *My Life and My All: The Life of St. Francis of Assisi*
Bruce Humphries, Publishers, Boston—Max Ehrmann, "Desiderata," in *The Poems of Max Ehrmann*
Mrs. Laura Huxley and Chatto & Windus Ltd.—Aldous Huxley, *The Perennial Philosophy*

Oxford and Cambridge University Presses—*New English Bible, New Testament*, Copyright © 1961

Alan Paton

Instrument
of Thy Peace

With a Foreword by Malcolm Muggeridge

Meditations prompted by the prayer of
St. Francis of Assisi
'Lord, make me an instrument of Thy peace.'

REVISED EDITION

Collins
Fount Paperbacks

First published by the Seabury Press, Inc.,
New York 1968
First issued in Fontana Books 1970
Reprinted in Fount Paperbacks 1977
Eleventh impression May 1980
Revised edition, March 1983
Second impression December 1985

Made and printed in Great Britain by
William Collins Sons & Co. Ltd, Glasgow

Foreword
by Malcolm Muggeridge

It is a rare privilege to be made privy, as one is in *Instrument of Thy Peace*, to the prayers and meditations of someone like Alan Paton. From his other writings—especially, of course, his most famous work, *Cry, the Beloved Country* —we know how he sees the world and his fellow men. (I deliberately, by the way, eschew the word "fiction" because, although Paton invents characters and situations, he is essentially a poet rather than a novelist; more a saint than either, maybe. An earthy saint, as poets are; in his case, rooted in the South African countryside he describes so enchantingly.) Again, as the dedicated and conscientious leader of a political party (now dissolved) in his native South Africa, his views on *apartheid* and other contemporary conflicts and dilemmas are public knowledge. Yet again, in his latest book—*Kontakion,* a beautiful and moving account of his marriage and his wife's death—we are told about a personal relationship, with all its ups and downs, stresses and strains, which enriched and stabilised his life.

All this we know. Yet there is something else. Paton is, above all, a religious man, a Christian believer. Everything he has done and thought has borne some relation to this circumstance. It is the private, interior, Christian life of Paton which finds expression in his commentary on one of the most wonderful prayers ever addressed to God—that of St. Francis of Assisi beginning: "Lord, make me an instrument of Thy peace." The result is a devotional work of exceptional quality fit to stand beside Simone Weil's

Waiting on God and Bonhoeffer's *Letters and Papers from Prison.*

I choose these two books deliberately. Just as the background to Bonhoeffer's is the fact that he was in prison in a Germany rapidly going down to defeat under the crazed leadership of Hitler and his Nazis, and to Simone Weil's the humiliation of France and her own impending exile, so the inescapable background to *Instrument of Thy Peace* is Paton's residence in South Africa and relationship to the South African authorities. He, too, might well have gone into exile, and been an honoured figure in this country or America. Had he done so, he still would have loved St. Francis's prayer, but the poignancy would have been less. Leaving, however, would have meant never returning. He decided to remain. We may think of him in his lovely but desolated land saying over to himself with an intensity of feeling intensified by the words' applicability in that place and in those circumstances: "Where there is hatred, let me sow love; where there is injury, pardon."

A Christian like Paton, is placed in an appallingly difficult and harrowing situation in South Africa today. On the one hand, the doctrine of *apartheid* is clearly opposed to the spirit and the teaching of the New Testament. No true Christian could possibly practise or uphold it. On the other hand, the forces of opposition to *apartheid* are, in the circumstances inevitably, violent, matching hatred with hatred and injury with injury rather than following St. Francis's quest for love and pardon. To add to the complexity, the Dutch Reformed Church itself preaches a biblical Christianity which finds a place for *apartheid* in the divine scheme of things.

Like many another, Paton might have become a zealot, looking forward to the day when the white oligarchs would be put down and a black leadership emerge to take control. This has happened in most of the former African colonial territories, not, it must be admitted, with particularly satisfactory results in terms of representative government or benign and just administration. In South Africa it would almost certainly be accompanied by bloodshed on a large scale, and result in *apartheid* in reverse, or black *apartheid*, with little scope for the propositions of St. Francis. Nonetheless, the overthrow of the existing regime, however achieved and whatever the consequences, might be considered an act of justice; even, to some, of Christian justice.

Equally, Paton might have taken a quiescent position, following St. Francis and his Divine Master in his personal ways and relationships, and leaving the drama of *apartheid* to work itself out on the stage of history till it reached its bloody and destructive climax. After all, Jesus himself deliberately refused to involve himself in the cause of Jewish nationalism. It would have been perfectly permissible for Paton likewise to contract out of the power struggle which is going on in South Africa between the black majority and the white minority, rendering to the South African Government his nominal acceptance of the obligations of citizenship and to God his Christian duty to love him and to love his neighbour as himself. It is not only in South Africa that a conflict exists between what is required of us as citizens and what is required of us as Christians. Such a conflict arises, to a greater or lesser degree of acerbity, wherever there is power and human beings exercising it—that's everywhere. In the circumstances of his time, it must have existed for St. Francis as it does for us today, and may even have been vaguely in his mind when he asked to be an instrument for sowing hope where there was despair, joy where there was sadness, light where there was darkness. Assuredly it is in Paton's mind when, with the utmost humility and reverence, he dedicates himself through St. Francis's prayer to these same purposes.

In *Instrument of Thy Peace* (and in *Kontakion*) one may see more clearly than in any of his other writings what it has cost Paton to steer this course between involvement and quiescence. It is so easy to hate; so easy to denounce, and call down curses, and wax indignant. So easy, too, to stand apart and offer reflections on the transience of all human authority, whether black, white or piebald. Reading between the lines a little, one senses how tired and dispirited Paton has sometimes been. There is a passing reference—in *Kontakion*, actually—to getting away from the world altogether; joining some religious community and leading an austere and brotherly existence there. One knows that feeling well enough. Again, the land itself! It has, indeed, a unique kind of passionate beauty, contrasted with an equally unique kind of evil. The golden harvest of the fields, and that other golden harvest torn out of the earth; Johannesburg and the splendid glowing valley reaching down to Cape Town. One could build a house on a high hill and sit quietly there talking with God. So Paton must often have thought; so it was within his power to do. Yet he has never done it, but stayed in the battle; is in it still.

Paton has for long seemed to me the particular hero in one of those truly desperate situations we humans know how to produce, not just out of our greed and wickedness (though they come into it, of course); also out of our very capacity for endurance and courage and disinterestedness of a sort. Paton sees and manages to convey all this, reaching far beyond the good guy–bad guy classification so dear to twentieth-century ideologues. It was my hope earlier this year to go to South Africa and record a conversation with him. Alas, in the event I was barred from entering the country, and as he is barred from coming out except for ever, we are unlikely ever to meet now. The best I can do is to pay this tribute to him, which I consider it a great honour to have been asked to do.

Had our conversation been possible, I had planned to raise with him precisely the question he deals with so perceptively in *Instrument of Thy Peace*; namely, how we are to balance our duties and responsibilities as citizens of this world with keeping clearly in view the kingdom not of this world which Christ came to proclaim. To St. Francis it all seemed perfectly clear. The hopes and desires of this world

8

were a fantasy on which he turned his back when the reality of Christ's other kingdom became apparent to him. He loved poverty and the poor, as he did the sun and the moon and all creation, and even the death of the body; but he never, as far as I know, concerned himself with the laws which made some serfs and some freemen, some rich and some poor, some to command and some to obey.

Any such position today is suspect, though not, praise God, the love and charity that go with it. The inevitability, and even necessity, of conflict is taken for granted, and in South Africa—one of its harshest arenas—the battle lines are drawn between naked Black and White Power, with no place for Paton's liberal contingent, except, maybe, as decoys on one side or the other. So we await the outcome, with dread or exaltation or stoical indifference, but with little doubt as to what it will be. I daresay the very obduracy of the Afrikaaners, their stubborn refusal to alter by a hairbreadth the course on which they are set, is due to a conscious or unconscious awareness that it is leading infallibly to *Götterdämmerung*.

Yet still, as Paton shows, even in these drastic circumstances St. Francis's prayer remains valid, if only as a focus for the doubts and questioning to which history's overbearing ways give rise. There is a world beyond history, as there is a hope beyond both victory and defeat and a love beyond justice. When St. Francis turned aside from the pursuit of happiness to the pursuit of God he signalised the occasion by embracing a leper. This was not a dramatic gesture designed to overcome his repugnance for the leper's rotting flesh, but a joyous recognition that he had found in him a beloved brother. In other words, equality (which is what all our earthly conflicts are ultimately about) resides, not in the overthrowing of oppressors and the triumph of justice, but in the recognition that we are all members of one family whose father is in heaven. So St. Francis's prayer magnificently concludes with the everlasting promise that in giving we receive, in pardoning we are pardoned, and in

9

dying we are born again to everlasting life. Words which Paton dares to echo and expound in his own beautiful and sincere way across the stricken battlefield his beloved country has become.

Prologue

This book is written for sinners, and by one of them. It is written for those who wish with all their hearts to be better, purer, less selfish, more useful; for those who do not wish to be cold in love, and who know that being cold in love is perhaps the worst sin of all; for those who wish to keep their faith bright and burning in a dark and faithless world; for those who seek not so much to lean on God as to be the active instruments of his peace.

I wrote also for those who are inclined to melancholy, for those who are inclined to withdraw rather than to participate, for those who are tempted to retreat into pietism because they are afraid of active engagement in the world, for those who deceive themselves that to be pious is to be more faithful to the gospel than to concern themselves with the building of a more just order of society.

I believe I shall be able to help some of them, not so much out of my own strength, which is not considerable, but out of the strength of one of the greatest, sweetest, and purest of the disciples, St. Francis of Assisi, who in his turn drew his strength from his Divine Master.

More and more as time goes by, the memory of Francis of Assisi comes to be treasured by the whole Christian world. Christians disagree about many things, but they seldom, perhaps never, disagree about

St. Francis. It is impossible for any Christian to hear or read or pray the immortal "Lord, make me an instrument of Thy peace," and not realise that he or she is in the presence of holiness.

It was nearly fifteen years ago that *Instrument of Thy Peace* was written. It was written during a time of great stress and anxiety. My wife Dorrie, to whom I had been married for thirty-nine years, was dying, slowly and painfully, of the terrible complaint known as emphysema.

Although the book is fifteen years old, it still speaks to me clearly. I can come to only one conclusion, that I was given help to write it. I can only relate the strange experience that as I re-read it, there are parts of it that help and move me as though some other hand had written them.

Alan Paton
12 October 1981

Instrument
of Thy
Peace

Lord, make me an instrument of Thy peace. Where there is hatred, let me sow love; where there is injury, pardon; where there is doubt, faith; where there is despair, hope; where there is sadness, joy; where there is darkness, light.

O Divine Master, grant that I may not so much seek to be consoled, as to console; not so much to be understood, as to understand; not so much to be loved, as to love. For it is in giving that we receive, it is in pardoning that we are pardoned, it is in dying that we are born again to eternal life.

1

Lord, make me an instrument of Thy peace.

PRAYER OF ST. FRANCIS

We pray for many things, for loved ones, for one sick, for one dying, for health, for much-needed money, for success in examinations, for our country, for the peace of the world. We pray for forgiveness of sins, for conquest of one particular sin that defeats us, for help in some situation that frightens or threatens us. We pray especially hard—most of us—when our own safety or security is threatened.

Sometimes we cannot pray, because we are fallen into a melancholy, and therefore have for the time lost our hope and our faith, and have no one to pray to.

I myself have done this, but now I wish to place on record that I am in unrepayable debt to Francis of Assisi, for when I pray his prayer, or even remember it, my melancholy is dispelled, my self-pity comes to an end, my faith is restored, because of this majestic conception of what the work of a disciple should be.

So majestic is this conception that one dare no longer be sorry for oneself. This world ceases to be one's enemy and becomes the place where one lives and works and serves. Life is no longer nasty, mean, brutish, and short, but becomes the time that one needs to make it less nasty and mean, not only for others, but indeed also for oneself.

We are brought back instantaneously to the reality of our faith, that we are not passive recipients but active instruments. The right relationship between man and God is instantly restored.

Francis of Assisi no doubt often prayed for something for himself, or for the order he had founded, or for the chapel and huts at Porziuncola. But in his prayer he asks nothing for himself, or perhaps he asks everything, and that is that his whole life, all his gifts, his physical strength, shall be an instrument in God's hand.

And I say to myself, this is the only way in which a Christian can encounter hatred, injury, despair, and sadness, and that is by throwing off his helplessness and allowing himself to be made the bearer of love, the pardoner, the bringer of hope, the comforter of those that grieve. And I believe that if you allow yourself to be so made, you will be so.

I think as I write this of a man who is leaving prison to return to the world. During these years he has paid more attention to religion than ever before in his life. As he leaves, the prison chaplain assures him that the past is done, the past is forgiven. But when he returns to the world, he finds that the world has not forgiven, that it has not forgotten his past. So hope changes to despair, faith to doubt. It seems that God has not forgiven him after all.

It is here that a great duty falls upon us all, to be the bearers of God's forgiveness, to be the instrument of his love, to be active in compassion. This man's return to the world is made tragic because *we were not there*. God moves in his own mysterious ways, but a great deal of the time he moves through us. And it is because we are not there that so many do not believe in God's love.

JESUS: He came to the disciples and found them asleep; and he said to Peter, "What! Could none of you stay awake with me one hour?"

JESUS: You are salt to the world. And if salt becomes tasteless, how is its saltness to be restored?

DAG HAMMARSKJOLD (to himself on the eve of a meeting of the Security Council): Your responsibility is indeed terrifying. If you fail, it is God, thanks to your having betrayed Him, who will fail mankind. You fancy you can be responsible *to* God; can you carry the responsibility *for* God?

O Lord, help us to be masters of ourselves, that we may be servants of others.

> SIR ALEXANDER PATERSON
> (who devoted his life and great talents to
> the reform of British prisons and institutions
> for delinquent boys and girls)

O Lord, open my eyes that I may see the need of others, open my ears that I may hear their cries, open my heart so that they need not be without succour, let me be not afraid to defend the weak because of the anger of the strong, nor afraid to defend the poor because of the anger of the rich. Show me where love and hope and faith are needed, and use me to bring them to those places. And so open my eyes and my ears that I may this coming day be able to do some work of peace for Thee.

2

No one is too weak, too vile, too unimportant, to be God's instrument.

⤙ And Moses said unto God, Who am I, that I should go unto Pharaoh, and that I should bring forth the children of Israel out of Egypt?

And the Lord said unto Moses, Certainly I will be with thee; and this shall be a token unto thee, that I have sent thee: When thou hast brought forth the people out of Egypt, ye shall serve God upon this mountain.

And Moses said unto the Lord, O my Lord, I am not eloquent, neither heretofore, nor since thou hast spoken unto thy servant: but I am slow of speech, and of a slow tongue.

And the Lord said unto him, Who hath made man's mouth? or who maketh the dumb, or deaf, or the seeing, or the blind? have not I, the Lord? Now therefore go, and I will be with thy mouth, and teach thee what thou shalt say.   *Exodus 3 and 4* KJV

No Christian should ever think or say that he is not fit to be God's instrument, for that in fact is what it means to be a Christian. We may be humble about many things, but we may never decline to be used. John the Baptist told the people by the river Jordan, "I baptise you with water, for repentance, but the one who comes after me is mightier than I, and I am not fit to take off his shoes." Then Jesus himself came to be baptised by him, and John tried to dissuade him, saying to him, "Do you come to me? I need rather to be baptised by you." Jesus replied, "Let it be so for the present; we do well to conform in this way with all that God requires." So John baptised him whose shoes he was not fit to take off.

The gospel is full of reassurances to us, some of them startling. You are salt to the world! You are light to all the world! Even the hairs of your head have all been counted! These words were exciting to those who heard them. Things might be dark but they were to be the light of the world. They were given a new sense of their value as persons. Especially was this true of women. One can hardly describe the joy of the first disciples, who were given by Jesus such a sense of their significance in the world. This same sense of significance has been given again and again to other people by disciples of Jesus. Of these none was greater than Francis of Assisi. He might well have prayed:

To those who have lost their way, let me restore it to them.

To those who are aimless, let me bring purpose.

To those who do not know who they are, let me teach them that they are the children of God and can be used as His instruments in the never-ending work of healing and redemption.

There are therefore two things for us to do. The first is never to doubt that God can use us if we are willing to be used, no matter what our weaknesses. The second is to see that God can use any other person who is willing to be used, whatever his weaknesses, and if need be, to assure him of this truth.

〜〜 One day as St. Francis was returning from his prayers in the wood, Brother Masseo met him, and wishing to test how humble he was, asked in a mocking manner, saying, "Why after thee? Why after thee? Why after thee?" St. Francis replied, "What is it thou wouldst say?" And Brother Masseo answered, "Say, why is it that all the world comes after thee, and everybody desires to see thee, and to hear thee, and to obey thee? Thou art not a man either comely of person, or of noble birth, or of great knowledge; whence then comes it that all the world runs after thee?"

Hearing this, St. Francis, filled with joy in his spirit, raised his face towards heaven, and remained for a great while with his mind lifted up to God; then returning to himself, he knelt down, and gave praise and thanks to God; and then, with great fervour of spirit, turning to Brother Masseo, he said, "Wouldst know why after me? Wouldst know why after me? Why all the world runs after me? This comes to me, because the eyes of the Most High God, which behold in all places both the evil and the good, even those most holy eyes have not seen amongst sinners one more vile, nor more insufficient, nor a greater sinner than I, and therefore to do that wonderful work which He intends to do, He hath not found on earth a viler creature than I; and for this cause He elected me to confound the nobility, and the grandeur, and the strength, and beauty, and wisdom of the world, that all men may know that all virtue and all goodness are of Him, and not of the creature, and that none should glory in his presence; but that he who glories should glory in the Lord, to whom is all honour and glory in eternity!"

Then Brother Masseo, at this humble and fervent reply, feared within himself, and knew certainly that St. Francis was grounded in humility.

THE LITTLE FLOWERS OF ST. FRANCIS OF ASSISI

Lord, make me willing to be used by Thee. May my knowledge of my unworthiness never make me resist being used by Thee. May the need of others always be remembered by me, so that I may ever be willing to be used by Thee.

And open my eyes and my heart that I may this coming day be able to do some work of peace for Thee.

3

Where there is hatred, let me sow love.

Let us leave aside for the time the immensely difficult question of what we are to do when we ourselves hate, when we ourselves are the objects of hatred, the immensely difficult question of how one can possibly love one's enemies. Let us also leave aside for the time the immensely difficult question of how we can possibly love those who are cruel or unjust or indifferent to others. Our Lord enjoined us to love our enemies, but one of the harshest judgments he ever passed was on the man who would cause a child to stumble.

The petition of St. Francis may be taken for the moment in an easier way, namely that he asks to be the reconciler of those who hate one another, or that he asks to be able to soften the heart of one who hates and to heal the grief and resentment and lostness of one who is hated. This is something that we can ask for ourselves. We can plead with those who hate, and encourage those who are hated; we can mediate between those who hate one another.

Yet this problem also will confront us with a great difficulty. A person who hates may find a transcendental reason (such as the love of Christ) why he should stop hating, and this transcendental reason becomes more important for him than his reasons for hating. This, of course, means that he undergoes a spiritual transformation, a conversion. But what of those who do not? How are we to help them? How are we to help people to find it easier not to hate?

William Temple wrote, "More potent than school or even than home, as a moral influence, is the whole structure of society and especially its economic structure. This fixes for all their place in the general scheme; and the way in which they gain and keep that place of necessity determines a great deal of their conduct and profoundly influences their outlook upon life."

To be the instrument of God's peace is not to confine oneself to the field of personal relationships, but to concern oneself also with the problems of human society, hunger, poverty, injustice, cruelty, exploitation, war.

Some Christians argue that if we would only change men, then society would change of itself. That there is some truth in this, none of us doubts. But the full truth is that we must try both to change man and to change society, and that there are some changes in man that cannot be achieved without some changes in society. The front is wider than that of pure evangelism.

Such a view arouses opposition, anger, even hatred, amongst antichange Christians. They call it the social gospel, and regard it as an adulteration of the teaching of Christ. With this opposition, this anger, even hatred, we shall have later to deal.

〜〜 It came to the ears of Francis that a bitter quarrel had arisen between the Bishop of Assisi and the city magistrates, and that bickering and anger were disfiguring the public life. Therefore Francis sent a message to the magistrates asking them to go at once to the Bishop's palace, and although they had all been excommunicated by the Bishop, they agreed out of veneration for Francis. Meanwhile Francis went to the palace, and as soon as the magistrates appeared, he and his brothers began to sing the "Canticle of the Sun." Hearing the singing, the Bishop came down to see what it was about, and as he came out of the door of the palace, the magistrates came in at the gate, and each eyed the other coldly.

Just as this happened, the brothers came to the new stanza which Francis had written for just this moment:

Praised be my Lord for those who for Thy love forgive
And weakness bear and tribulation
Blessed those who shall in peace endure,
For by Thee, most High, shall they be crowned.

Both Bishop and magistrates were humbled by these words, and when the canticle was done, they advanced to meet each other and were reconciled.

THE LITTLE FLOWERS OF ST. FRANCIS OF ASSISI

Behold, O Lord God, our strivings after a truer and more abiding order. Give us visions that bring back a lost glory to the earth, and dreams that foreshadow the better order which Thou hast prepared for us. Scatter every excuse of frailty and unworthiness: consecrate us all with a heavenly mission: open to us a clear prospect of our work. Give us strength according to our day gladly to welcome and gratefully to fulfil it, through Jesus Christ our Lord.

BISHOP WESTCOTT

Take all hate from my heart, O God, and teach me how to take it from the hearts of others. Open my eyes and show me what things in our society make it easy for hatred to flourish and hard for us to conquer it. Then help me to try to change these things.

And so open my eyes and my ears that I may this coming day be able to do some work of peace for Thee.

4

*Everyone who loves is a child of God and knows God, but
the unloving know nothing of God. For God is love.*

1 JOHN 4:7-8 NEB

This is a tremendous saying and it carries a most tremendous message to those who are faithful yet at times
are troubled by doubt, to those who are doubtful yet at
times are troubled by faith, it carries this tremendous message to those who already love Christ, but who are terrified
and appalled and bewildered by the great superstructure of
the beliefs and the theologies and the ordinances and the
disunities and the irrelevancies of Christianity and the
churches. I shall not easily forget reading Malcolm Muggeridge on the Crucifixion in the 1967 Easter Day issue of
The Observer. Mr. Muggeridge writes that he "can grasp
some sort of notion of a Deity, and of his loving purpose,
in which I, in common with all creation, am inextricably
enmeshed." But he cannot believe in the Virgin Birth, or
that Jesus was God's son "in any particular sense," or in
the Resurrection. He writes, "I even prefer to suppose that
some body-snatcher, accustomed to hang about Golgotha
to pick up anything that might be going, heard in his dim-

27

witted way that the King of the Jews was up for execution. Good! he thinks; there are bound to be pickings there. So he waits till the job is done, finds out where the corpse has been laid, drags the stones away, and then, making sure no one is watching, decamps with the body.

"What a disappointment for him! This King of the Jews has no crown, no jewels, no orbs, no sceptre, no ring; he is just a worthless, wasted, broken, naked body. The man contemptuously abandons the body to the vultures, who in their turn leave the bones to whiten in the sun.

"Those precious, precious bones!"

And I say to myself, what does one say to any person who wants to believe and who cannot believe (or who certainly cannot believe it all)? What does one say to one who loves Christ and cannot believe in the Virgin Birth or the Resurrection? What does one say to one who wants to believe that God is the kind of God that Jesus believed him to be, and who wants to worship him, but cannot accept the accumulation of creeds and articles and doctrines that seem in the eyes of the churches to be inseparable from God? What does one say to one who writes with such longing disbelief of those precious, precious bones, yet believes them to be only the bones of an ordinary man?

This problem is a real one. Was this wonderful man wonderful only when he taught morality, and not when he taught theology? Was his knowledge sound about man, and unsound about the divine and the supernatural? Was his life magnificent, but was he unsound on sex and marriage and divorce?

I myself no longer presume to answer these questions

with assurance. I cannot construct a body of belief that will be acceptable to all. Leslie Weatherhead, whose integrity I would never question, rejects miracle after miracle, and doctrine after doctrine, and then says that he believes in the Resurrection.

Is there nothing to hold on to? I believe there is, and it is that God is love, that if I love I am a child of God, and that if I am unloving I know not God. So I would say to those who love Christ and want to follow him, but are afraid of the doctrines and the theology, that they respond in all confidence to the call, "Take heart, it is I, do not be afraid."

He came and took me by the hand
Up to a red rose tree,
He kept his meaning to Himself
But gave a rose to me.
I did not pray Him to lay bare
The mystery to me,
Enough the rose was Heaven to smell
And His own face to see.

RALPH HODGSON

O Lord, perfect for me that which is lacking of Thy gifts: of faith, increase my littleness of faith; of hope, establish trembling hope; of love, kindle its smoking flame; shed abroad Thy love in my heart, withal to love Thee, my friend in Thee, mine enemy for Thee. Let me fear one thing only, the fearing aught more than Thee.

LANCELOT ANDREWES

O God, Creator of mankind, I do not aspire to comprehend You or Your creation, nor to understand pain or suffering. I aspire only to relieve the pain and suffering of others, and I trust that in doing so, I may understand more clearly Your nature, that You are the Father of all mankind, and that the hairs of my head are numbered.

And help me this coming day to do some work of peace for You.

5

Where there is doubt, let me sow faith.

PRAYER OF ST. FRANCIS

St. Francis is not here referring to that kind of doubt that accompanies the search for truth. He refers to doubt of God's love and goodness, which was one of the great themes of the teaching of Jesus.

↬ When they came back to the disciples they saw a large crowd surrounding them and lawyers arguing with them. As soon as they saw Jesus the whole crowd were overcome with awe, and they ran forward to welcome him. He asked them, "What is this argument about?" A man in the crowd spoke up: "Master, I brought my son to you. He is possessed by a spirit which makes him speechless. Whenever it attacks him, it dashes him to the ground, and he foams at the mouth, grinds his teeth, and goes rigid. I asked your disciples to cast it out, but they failed." Jesus answered: "What an unbelieving and perverse generation! How long shall I be with you? How long must I endure you? Bring him to me." So they brought the boy to him; and as soon as the spirit saw him it threw the boy into convulsions, and he fell on the ground and rolled about foaming at the mouth. Jesus asked his father, "How long has he been like this?" "From childhood," he replied; "often it has tried to make an end of him by throwing him into the fire or into water. But if it is at all possible for you, take pity upon us and help us." "If it is possible!" said Jesus. "Everything is possible to one who has faith." "I have faith," cried the boy's father; "help me where faith falls short."   *Mark 9:14–24* NEB

I have faith; help me where faith falls short! Or as the older Bible had it, Lord I believe, help thou mine unbelief.

That indeed is the cry of many of us, for our faith is many times put to the test, by the failure of our ideals to triumph, by the long illness of some beloved person, by world disasters, by wars and rumours of wars. "Why does God allow it?" is a question one often hears. "Is God really a loving God when he permits such things to happen?" "Can God really be all-powerful? For if he is all-powerful, then he cannot be loving."

Sometimes these questions are asked by people who want to rid themselves of the belief in God, but sometimes they are asked by people who want to keep their faith in God, and who hope for reassuring answers to these disturbing questions.

As far as we know, Francis of Assisi never asked himself these questions. If there was sorrow, he asked to be allowed to bring joy. If there was darkness, he asked to be allowed to bring light. If there was grief, he asked to be allowed to bring comfort. This concept of discipleship

32

was sublime. If the creation groaned and travailed until now, then he would not question, but would devote himself to the relieving of its pain and the assuaging of its grief.

There is even more to it than this, for in taking upon himself the sorrow of the world, as his own Master had done before him, he was a living witness to the activity of God's love in the world. God's love, though it is not limited to us as instruments, nevertheless uses us as instruments, so that those who are in need of it, find it in us. It is possible that some will never find it if they do not find it in us. And it is also possible that some will not believe in it, because they do not find it in us. "If *you* are a follower of Christ," they say, "I want no part of him."

So the matters of faith and of love are seen to be inseparable. If we do not love, then others will not have faith.

⤷ Philip said to him, "Lord, show us the Father and we ask no more." Jesus answered, "Have I been all this time with you, Philip, and you still do not know me? Anyone who has seen me has seen the Father. Then how can you say, 'Show us the Father'? Do you not believe that I am in the Father, and the Father in me? I am not myself the source of the words I speak to you, it is the Father who dwells in me doing his own work."

John 14:8–10 NEB

⤷ I give you a new commandment: love one another; as I have loved you, so you are to love one another. If there is this love among you, then all will know that you are my disciples.   *John 13:34–35* NEB

⌐ By this shall all men know that ye are my disciples, if ye have love one to another.   *John 13:35* KJV

Help me, O Lord, to be more loving. Help me, O Lord, not to be afraid to love the outcast, the leper, the unmarried pregnant woman, the traitor to the State, the man out of prison. Help me by my love to restore the faith of the disillusioned, the disappointed, the early bereaved. Help me by my love to be the witness of Thy love.

And may I this coming day be able to do some work of peace for Thee.

6

Forgive us our trespasses, as we forgive them that trespass against us.

JESUS

Repent, for the Kingdom of Heaven is upon you.

ST. JOHN

The fully forgiven man does not rejoice in his own forgiveness but in the divine love to which he owes it; and his past sin persists in his experience no longer as a source of shame but as the occasion of a new wonder in his adoration of the love divine.

WILLIAM TEMPLE

He who is able to love himself is able to love others also; he who has learned to overcome self-contempt has overcome his contempt for others.

PAUL TILLICH

It is in pardoning that we are pardoned.

ST. FRANCIS

It was thirty years ago at a penal-reform congress in Johannesburg that I first encountered the extraordinary theological view that when a man commits an offence he rends the moral order of the universe, and that this damage is repaired only by his punishment. This extraordinary theology underlay much of our penal practice in South African courts and prisons at that time.

This theory was discarded in respect of juvenile offenders in 1934, and later in respect of adult first offenders, but it still prevails in our ordinary prisons, though even there a system of gradual relaxation of restrictions is applied.

The sequence "offence-punishment" was once considered complete. The punishment cancelled out the offence in some mysterious way, even when the offender had for the rest of his life to declare his offence on certain official documents, such as an application for a passport. Even more baffling was the question of what happened to the moral order of the universe when the offender was never caught.

The Christian sequence is quite different. It runs "offence-forgiveness-restoration." It is doubtful even whether repentance is an essential term in the sequence. In the story of the woman taken in adultery, Jesus says to her, "Neither do I condemn thee, go thou and sin no more," but whether she repented or not we do not know. In his injunction that we should love our enemies, and pray for them that despitefully use us, there is no mention of their repentance, and in fact the implication is that they do not repent. *We must therefore learn to forgive unconditionally*. We must even eschew the use of that fascinating statement, *I forgive but I do not forget*.

The sequence is, however, quite different when we

ourselves are the offenders. Whether God requires repentance before he forgives, I do not presume to know. But I presume to know that for us ourselves, repentance is essential before we can feel forgiven, and this seems to be the belief of the Church also.

I should like to write a few words for those who *have* repented, and who *have* been forgiven (whether in private or public confession, or by the person whom they have harmed), but who still *cannot feel forgiven.*

There is something wrong with you. You are literally not understanding the gospel. You are not understanding the injunction of Jesus to you that you must not forgive your brother seven times, but seventy times seven. For if you are expected to do that, what do you think God may be expected to do? What is more, you are making it difficult, if not impossible, for God to use you as an instrument, because of your feeling of guilt for something that has been forgiven. Paul Tillich, in his great sermon "You Are Accepted," says that what we have to do is simply to accept the fact that we are accepted. Beloved, now are ye the sons of God; it doth not yet appear what ye shall be. Tillich says: "But sometimes it happens that we receive the power to say 'Yes' to ourselves, that peace enters into us and makes us whole, that self-hate and self-contempt disappear and that our self is reunited with itself. Then we say that grace has come upon us."

There is a well-known saying, "I am at peace with the world," but it is much more important to be able to say, "I am at peace with myself." In the poem "Desiderata," by Max Ehrmann, there is the wise admonition: "Beyond a wholesome discipline, be gentle with yourself."

◠◠ For many men and women believe that God is All-Mighty and may do all; and that He is All-Wisdom and can do all; but that He is All-Love and will do all—there they stop short.

And it is this lack of knowing that most hinders God's lovers. For when they begin to hate sin, and to amend them by the ordinance of Holy Church, yet there dwells a dread that stirs them to beholding of themselves and of their sins before done. And this dread they take for a meekness; but this is a foul blindness, and a weakness if we cannot despise it. For if we knew it that, we should suddenly despise it, as we do another sin that we know; for it comes of the enemy, and it is against the truth.

For all the properties of the blessed Trinity, it is God's will that we have most sureness in liking and love. For Love makes Might and Wisdom full meek to us. For right as by the courtesy of God He forgets our sins when we repent, right so will He that we forget our sin, and all our heaviness, and all our doubtful dreads.

LADY JULIAN OF NORWICH

FREDERICK MACNUTT: O Lord, forgive me for what I have been, sanctify what I am, and order what I shall be.

THE BOOK OF COMMON PRAYER: We acknowledge and bewail our manifold sins and wickedness, Which we, from time to time, most grievously have committed, by thought, word, and deed, Against thy Divine Majesty. . . .

THE BOOK OF COMMON PRAYER: Almighty God . . . have mercy upon you; pardon and deliver you from all your sins; confirm and strengthen you in all goodness; and bring you to everlasting life; through Jesus Christ our Lord.

Lord, let no unnecessary sense of guilt prevent me from being used by Thee, let not the knowledge of my unworthiness prevent me from being used by Thee. Lord, never let the forgiven past prevent me from being used by Thee.

And may I this coming day be able to do some work of peace for Thee.

7

Where there is despair, let me bring hope.

PRAYER OF ST. FRANCIS

There is no more terrible condition of the soul than despair. In a way it brings life to an end, yet we continue to breathe, to eat, and to drink. But we hope no more.

When we despair, most of us cannot turn our faces to the wall and die. Even our despair does not destroy our sense of duty (except in extreme cases). If we have dependents, we must continue to work. But in the old monasteries, those who did not perform work were in danger of lapsing into sloth, often called *accidie* or *acedia*. This is not an extreme form of laziness as some suppose, but the dark night of the soul. There is nothing to live for, fight for, pray for. In earlier days it was counted one of the seven deadly sins, and although we have today a fuller understanding of it, it is important to note that even in despair we are not absolved from responsibility, not only for others, but for ourselves.

Sometimes an external event brings on despair. The work of a lifetime may be destroyed in a moment. An outbreak of war destroys the lifelong work of a man for peace.

A cyclone ruins in a few moments a man's farm, destroys his house, kills his cattle, lays waste his crops, takes away his soil.

Sometimes the external event is so terrible that hardly one of us would not despair. But sometimes the external event is not visible to others. Some people fall into a despair over the irredeemable wickedness of man, whereas we know that man is not irredeemably wicked. It would seem that in most cases of despair, there is also in us a predisposition to despair. Some escape despair by way of cynicism, but one imagines that St. Francis would have prayed for cynics also.

And here it should be recorded that St. Francis himself passed through a period of despair lasting two years. One of his biographers, Father Isidore O'Brien, attributed this to the fear that his rule of poverty would be modified, to his disillusionment over the gross behaviour of many of the Crusaders, and to his increasing physical blindness. Yet clearly there was something deeply wrong in himself. He withdrew from the world, he who had asked to be the instrument of God's peace. He visited no more the convent of the Poor Clares, lest it should be a source of scandal. It was Clare herself who used all her holiness and skill to restore him to himself. She appealed to him to visit them and not forsake them. The visit was a failure. He did not preach to them as was his custom. Instead, he sprinkled ashes upon his head and recited the psalm, *Miserere mei, Deus*. Then he left them.

But Clare would not accept defeat. In Father O'Brien's significant words, she saw that "Francis needed human help to draw him out of himself." She next asked to be allowed to dine with the brothers at Porziuncola, and so great was her insistence that Francis could not deny her.

〜〜 When Clare arrived at the Portiuncula, she went into the chapel of St. Mary of the Angels, and devoutly saluted the Virgin Mary, before whose altar her hair had been cut off when she received the veil. Meanwhile Francis set out the meal on the bare ground, as was his custom. Then he and one of the brothers, and Clare and the sister who had accompanied her, sat down together, surrounded by the rest of the brothers, sitting humbly round them. When the first dish was served, Francis began to speak of God so sweetly, so sublimely, and in a manner so wonderful, that the grace of God fell upon them all, and all were rapt in Christ.

Now the people of Assisi and Bettona, and of all the country around about, saw St. Mary of the Angels as it were on fire, with the convent and the woods adjoining. The people of Assisi hastened with great speed to put out the fire, but on arriving they saw no fire, only Francis and Clare and all their companions sitting around their humble meal on the ground. Then they knew that what they had seen was a celestial fire.

THE LITTLE FLOWERS OF ST. FRANCIS OF ASSISI

It was not only Clare who helped Francis out of his despair, nor did his despair end merely because the Pope approved his amended rule of poverty. He heard Christ, by way of rebuke, say to him (and to some of us):

"Why art thou distressed? Have I so set thee a shepherd over My religion that thou knowest not I am its chief Protector? I set thee over it, a simple man, to the end that those who will, may follow thee in those things I work in thee for an example to others. It is I who have called them; I who will keep and feed them; and I will make

43

good the falling away of some by putting others in their place, in such wise that if these others be not born I will cause them to be born."

What part Francis himself played in his own liberation, it is hard to determine. But many writers on despair believe that the person in despair must himself help to liberate himself. He can be helped by others by the grace of God, but his own action is required.

John Keble advised, "When you find yourself overpowered as it were by melancholy, the best way is to go out, and do something kind to somebody or other."

Adela M. Curtis wrote (in *The Way of Silence*): "If you have a negative feeling (worry, fear, anxiety, hate, resentment) and it does not go away when you meditate, you must take immediate action. . . .

"Instead of sitting down in front of that mood to wrestle with it by denials, *do* an heroic thing . . . make yourself act quickly on the opposite side of that state. . . .

"You have no idea of the virtue of acting on what you know is right if you want to overcome your feelings or nerves. There is some fear in it too. It ought to appeal to your sporting instincts."

What simple advice to relieve the darkest illness of the soul! And I believe it is right. I give my own testimony that when I am tempted to despair, that when I am tempted to believe in the futility of all endeavour, that when I believe that the love of God is not actively helping me, I pray or speak or read this prayer of St. Francis, which is the subject of these meditations, and I decide to act on it, or I should rather say, *I am moved to act on it*. From that moment the temptation to despair is ended. Therefore I am in this unrepayable debt.

When his life's work was threatened, St. Ignatius of Loyola was asked what he would do if Pope Paul IV dissolved or otherwise acted against the Society of Jesus, to which he had devoted his energy and gifts; and he replied: "I would pray for fifteen minutes, then I would not think of it again."

Lord, save me from despair, and if I am in despair, make me to do some work of peace for Thee.

8

*Therefore I bid you put away anxious thoughts about food
and drink . . . , and clothes to cover your body. Surely
life is more than food, the body more than clothes. Look
at the birds of the air; they do not sow and reap and store
in barns, yet your heavenly Father feeds them. You are
worth more than the birds! Is there a man of you who by
anxious thought can add a foot to his height? And why be
anxious about clothes? Consider how the lilies grow in the
fields; they do not work, they do not spin; and yet, I tell
you, even Solomon in all his splendour was not attired like
one of these.* MATTHEW 6:25–29 NEB

This is not one of the easiest passages in the Gospels.
Nor am I necessarily a suitable person to write about these
particular anxieties because I do not have them. I have
known men sacked, fired from their jobs in middle age, at
that very time of life when it is hard for a man to get another. Our own duty in such cases is plain, and that is to
show friendship and to give what help will be accepted.
But what else can we say to the anxious man? Can we
say to him that he is worth more than the birds, when we

know that more people suffer today from hunger and poverty than ever before in the history of man?

Can we say to the parents of teenagers in this modern world that they should not be anxious? Can we say to the parents of a son or daughter who is travelling in a plane that has gone silent over the sea or the mountains, that they should not be anxious? Of course we can not. There is only one thing that one can do in such cases of anxiety, and that is to pray for one's friends and to show one's friendship towards them.

(I have a friend who has said to me on more than one occasion, "You must not worry, I *know* everything will be all right." I think his statement is absurd, and I could not make it myself to another. But I know he is trying to comfort me, and I love him for that. I think on the whole I would prefer him to a friend who said, "You must hope for the best, but you must prepare for the worst." However, I don't really know. I think it would depend on the way my friends said it!)

I do not think Jesus is teaching us about particular cases of anxiety. I think he is teaching us not to be *anxious persons*. And he strongly suggests in this passage that this anxiousness in us is caused because our scale of values is wrong. I have a friend, a good woman; a faithful churchwoman, who is perpetually anxious; yet her life has been characterised by what appears to me to be continuous happiness. She appears to me to be not thankful enough for what *has happened* to her, and instead to be overanxious about what *might happen* to her.

We ourselves who are not anxious persons can well act in the spirit of Francis, which is the spirit of Christ, towards those who are. Our duty is clear. And for those who are overanxious, they must face the truth that their faith in the God whom Jesus taught, who is indeed our Father, is not adequate, and that there is no point in believing in the Christian God at all if we do not believe that we are in his care. And they must also face the truth that if they are overanxious, they cannot be of much help to others.

〜〜 A tale that I knew in my childhood: The inn was full, and the innkeeper sent the maid down to the cellar to draw more ale. When after much time she had not appeared, the innkeeper went down to the cellar to see what had happened to her. There she was sitting weeping before the cask, while the ale was running to waste. The innkeeper quickly closed the tap and said angrily to her, "What is this all about?"

With tearful eyes she pointed to the beam above the cask, on which was lying a hammer.

"I was thinking, master," she said, "one day my little daughter may be working at the inn, and she may be sent down here to draw the ale, and the hammer may fall on her head and kill her."

JOHN BUNYAN: Looking very narrowly before him as he went, he espied two lions in the way. Now, thought he, I see the dangers that Mistrust and Timorous were driven back by. Then he was afraid, and thought also himself to go back after them, for he thought nothing but death was before him. But the porter at the lodge, whose name is Watchful, perceiving that Christian made a halt as if he would go back, cried unto him saying, "Is thy strength so small? Fear not the lions, for they are chained, and are placed there for trial of faith where it is, and for discovery of those that have none: keep in the midst of the path, and no hurt shall come unto thee."

However, one cannot make light of deep and persistent anxiety. Dr. James Reid tells of a man who suffered from period attacks of acute anxiety, which prayer did not seem to help. In one of his dark moments he went to a friend, who advised him to commit himself to God, even if he had to accept his recurrent fear as a wounded soldier accepts his disability. The result, writes Dr. Reid, was gradual, but in the end there was a total release.

To commit oneself to God is to make oneself an instrument of his peace. In acting for him we do not have so much time to worry about ourselves. In the end we may cease to worry about ourselves altogether.

Jesus gave advice to people who are too anxious:

"Set your mind on God's Kingdom and His justice before everything else, and all the rest will come to you as well. So do not be anxious about tomorrow; tomorrow will look after itself. Each day has troubles enough of its own." (Matthew 6:34 NEB)

"Set your troubled hearts at rest. Trust in God always; trust also in me." (John 14:1 NEB)

O Lord, save us from anxiety, and if we are anxious let us commit ourselves to You more fully, to be used as the instruments of Your peace, so that we learn to be less concerned about ourselves and more concerned about others.

And may we this coming day be able to do some work of peace for You.

9

Then he went out and made his way as usual to the Mount of Olives, accompanied by the disciples. When he reached the place he said to them, "Pray that you may be spared the hour of testing." He himself withdrew from them about a stone's throw, knelt down, and began to pray: "Father, if it be thy will, take this cup away from me. Yet not my will but thine be done."

And now there appeared to him an angel from heaven bringing him strength, and in anguish of spirit he prayed the more urgently; and his sweat was like clots of blood falling to the ground.

When he rose from prayer and came to the disciples he found them asleep, worn out by grief. "Why are you sleeping?" he said. "Rise and pray that you may be spared the test." LUKE 22:39–46 NEB

This is one of the most wonderful passages in the Gospels because it shows that Jesus was not God pretending to be a man. In the garden of Gethsemane, Jesus told Peter and James and John that his soul was "exceeding sorrowful unto death," which the New English Bible renders "my heart is ready to break with grief." The English Revised Version says that Jesus "began to be sore amazed, and to be very heavy," which the New English Bible renders "horror and dismay came over him." According to St. Luke, he asked that if it were God's will, he should be spared the Cross. According to St. Matthew, he asked to be spared "if it is possible." According to the first three Gospels, he concluded his petition with the words "Thy will be done," or more strongly, "yet not my will but Thine be done."

What was happening there in Gethsemane? I am not a theologian or a learned scholar, but it seems plain to me that Jesus was filled with fear of his impending death; it was the first time in his life, so far as we know, that he had been afraid. A short time before he had told his disciples not to let their hearts be troubled, yet now his own heart was ready to break with grief. More than once he had told his disciples that he must die; now he asked God not to let him die.

The story is not finished yet. He suddenly rises from the ground, and goes to his sleeping disciples and says to them, "The hour has come." When Judas comes with the soldiers, he does not resist. He says, "Let the scriptures be fulfilled." To the man who strikes at the High Priest's servant, he says, "Put up your sword. All who take the sword shall die by the sword." He then says those strange words, "Do you suppose that I cannot appeal to my Father, who would at once send to my aid more than twelve legions of angels?" But he adds that this cannot be.

To me as a writer this is an unsurpassable picture of a man struggling with God and with destiny, all in the framework of a great obedience. So do we all struggle, and though not always with the same obedience, we wish it might be so.

During the trial the struggle seems to have ceased for a while. Indeed, after the trial, on the Via Dolorosa, he turns to the women mourning and lamenting, and says "do not weep for me; no, weep for yourselves and your children." (St. Luke) In the physical agony of the Cross he remembered his mother (St. John), but in the spiritual agony that accompanies it he utters that loud and desolate cry, "Eli, Eli, lama sabachthani?" which is interpreted, "My God, My God, why hast Thou forsaken me?" (St. Matthew; St. Mark)

This story is not finished yet. According to St. John he again cries out aloud, and this time he says, "It is finished," meaning, it is accomplished.

And according to St. Luke he gives up his life with the words, "Into Thy hands I commend my spirit."

So there it all is, an agony of grief and fear, a rousing of oneself to face the ultimate ordeal, an act of peace to repair an act of violence, a remembrance under sentence of death of the women of Jerusalem and of his mother, one cry of utter desolation, and another that the work is finished, a commending of himself into the hands of God.

No wonder that Francis of Assisi so loved this man, and followed him as his Lord and Brother. For if there has to be grief, if there has to be fear, if there has to be desolation, let there also be a continuous remembrance of others, a finishing, a commending of one's spirit into the hands of God. For the first is a wound, and the second is a healing. The first is a judgment on life, the second is a vindication. The first is a curse, the second is a benediction. Even so, Lord, may it be with us.

᭼᭼ *The Leper on the Umbrian Plain:* One day Francis was riding on the Umbrian Plain, on his way home to Assisi. Though he too was struggling with God and destiny, he was still a rich man's son, and was fashionably dressed and riding a gaily caparisoned horse. Then suddenly his horse shied under him, and he looked up to see the sight that he most feared in all the world, a leper. Then happened for him, as for us also, a tremendous event, for Francis, fighting down his loathing and his fear, dismounted from his horse, and going to the leper, put money into his hand. Then impelled by some power that had overcome his fear, he took the hand and kissed it, putting his lips to the leper's flesh. And the leper, seeing that Francis was afire with love, took hold of him and gave him the kiss of peace and Francis kissed him also. Then Francis mounted his horse and rode back to Assisi with joy. From that day onwards he began to visit the lepers in the lazar house of Assisi, bringing them gifts and kissing their hands. He wrote in his will, "the Lord Himself led me amongst them, and I showed mercy to them, and when I left them, what had seemed bitter to me was changed into sweetness of body and soul."

THE LITTLE FLOWERS OF ST. FRANCIS OF ASSISI

A Legend: Francis remounted his horse and rode away. Then suddenly he turned round, but there was no one to be seen on the road at all. Then he knew that he had kissed the Lord.

ALDOUS HUXLEY: Fear cannot be got rid of by personal effort, but only by the ego's absorption in a cause greater than its own interests. Absorption in any cause will rid the mind of some of its fears; but only absorption in the loving and knowing of the divine Ground can rid it of *all* fear. For when the cause is less than the highest, the sense of fear and anxiety is transferred from the self to the cause—as when heroic self-sacrifice for a loved individual or institution is accompanied by anxiety in regard to that for which the sacrifice is made. Whereas if the sacrifice is made for God, and for others for God's sake, there can be no fear or abiding anxiety, since nothing can be a menace to the divine Ground, and even failure and disaster are to be accepted as being in accord with the divine will.

O Lord, into Thy hands I commend my spirit, and the spirits of all those whom I love. Into Thy hands I commend the spirits of all those who are fearful, of death or life, of principalities or powers, of things present or of things that may never come. Into Thy hands I commend the spirits of all those who fear change, more than they fear Thee, who put the law above justice, and order above love.

And help me this coming day to do some work of peace for Thee.

10

There is no fear in love; perfect love banishes fear.

1 JOHN 4:18 NEB

The wisdom of the words of Aldous Huxley in the preceding meditation is profound. Only when our cause is the highest cause, will all fear be conquered. For if our cause is not the highest cause, if it is a nation or a party or a movement or a church, and if it is this with which we identify ourselves, then the defeat of our cause is the defeat of ourselves. But if we believe that God is the Ground of all being, we can accept defeat because in a sense we cannot be defeated.

The conquest of fear is therefore a tremendous consequence of trying to find out what God's cause is—and making it our own. But there may be another tremendous consequence also. We may come into conflict with those institutions which view with suspicion, and sometimes with active hostility, any persons who have a supreme loyalty which is above their loyalty to party or movement or state or church, even though each of these bodies may call itself Christian. There is many a nation in the world (or more accurately, there is many a national government in the world) that regards it as traitorous for a person to have a cause higher than that of the nation. If this nation calls itself Christian, it will argue that loyalty to God and loyalty to the nation are one and the same thing, and it will invent a Christian Nationalism in which one may have the best of both worlds. It will propound the proposition that only by being armed to the teeth can Christian civilisation preserve itself. It may propound the even more extraordinary proposition that self-preservation must be the first law of a Christian, for if Christians do not preserve themselves, how can Christianity be preserved?

I live in a country where most of the white citizens would claim to be Christians, would feel it to be their supreme duty to preserve their Christian civilisation, and sometimes, in moments of stress, would call it "White civilisation." Many of them believe that God placed them in southern Africa to carry out a "civilising mission." Most of them hold firmly the belief that this civilising mission can only be carried out by the separation from one another of all racial groups—residentially, educationally, culturally, politically, even religiously. I, for example, would have to receive a permit from the authorities if I wished to worship in a church which is situated in an African township or reserve, and this would only be granted for some special occasion. If I wished to worship there more often, it is almost certain that permission would be denied. Any Christian in South Africa who tried to break down the "middle wall of partition" between racial groups, or between persons of different racial groups, would find himself under suspicion, and this suspicion would vary directly as his zeal. Any Christian, or any other person, who tried to break down the political wall of partition would not only find himself under suspicion but might find himself house-arrested, or banned from attending any meeting, or limited to some small area, or banished to some remote area, or detained without trial for a period that might be extended for ever.

I write these words not with the trivial aim of bringing my government into disrepute, but with the aim of showing that if a Christian takes seriously the commandment to love his neighbour as himself, he may incur the active hostility of State and Church. And we should remember that Jesus did exactly that, and that he told his disciples that this might happen to them also. These sayings of Jesus should be taken seriously. Our Christian cause could well bring us into conflict with authority, and the only way in which we can overcome the fear of such a prospect is to believe that we are the instruments of God's peace, which means of course that we are the instruments of God's love, and because we are used by it, because it dwells in us, we have no cause for fear.

An Addendum: The thoughts just concluded above are complete, and I did not wish to damage the unity of them by adding any observation which was not part of the main theme. Yet there is one observation that is important to me, and I make it now.

The observation is this. We may well be chary of any person who makes the claim that his cause and God's cause are the same, who claims that he is in fact God's instrument. This claim may not be made explicitly, but may be implicit, as in the act of wearing a crucifix, or in the act of becoming a minister or priest, or in the act of accepting, say, office in the parish or diocese. How is one to judge such claims, whether explicit or implicit? How is one to judge such claimants? Is one able to do so? Yes, I believe one is, and the touchstone to use is the humility of the claimant. (But of the person or the church or the institution which makes such claims arrogantly, let us beware.)

At least one Christian showed this humility in an extraordinary way: After Francis had finally broken with his old life, and had stripped himself of his gay garments and handed them back to his father, declaring that he now had only one Father who was God, he was so filled with joy that he left Assisi and climbed up towards Gubbio, seeking the wildness and solitude and freedom of the mountains. Towards evening he happened by accident on a robbers' hideout, and they rushed out at him and demanded to know who he was, and what was his business. Full of joy he replied to them, "I am the herald of the Great King." So with loud laughter they stripped off the cloak that Bishop Guido had given him, and threw him into a snowdrift.

He crawled out of the snow, and dressed now only in his hairshirt, went singing on his way.

Give us courage, O Lord, to stand up and be counted, to stand up for those who cannot stand up for themselves, to stand up for ourselves when it is needful for us to do so. Let us fear nothing more than we fear Thee. Let us love nothing more than we love Thee, for thus we shall fear nothing also.

Let us have no other god before Thee, whether nation or party or state or church. Let us seek no other peace but the peace which is Thine, and make us its instruments, opening our eyes and our ears and our hearts, so that we should know always what work of peace we may do for Thee.

11

Hear the word of the Lord, ye rulers of Sodom; give ear unto the law of our God, ye people of Gomorrah.

To what purpose is the multitude of your sacrifices unto me? saith the Lord: I am full of the burnt offerings of rams, and the fat of fed beasts; and I delight not in the blood of bullocks, or of lambs, or of he goats.

When ye come to appear before me, who hath required this at your hand, to tread my courts?

Bring no more vain oblations; incense is an abomination unto me; the new moons and sabbaths, the calling of assemblies, I cannot away with; it is iniquity, even the solemn meeting.

Your new moons and your appointed feasts my soul hateth: they are a trouble unto me; I am weary to bear them.

And when ye spread forth your hands, I will hide mine eyes from you: yea, when ye make many prayers, I will not hear: your hands are full of blood.

Wash you, make you clean; put away the evil of your doings from before mine eyes; cease to do evil.

Learn to do well; seek judgment, relieve the oppressed, judge the fatherless, plead for the widow.

Come now, and let us reason together, saith the Lord:

though your sins be as scarlet, they shall be as white as snow; though they be red like crimson, they shall be as wool. ISAIAH 1:10–18 KJV

Then shall the King say unto them on his right hand, Come, ye blessed of my Father, inherit the Kingdom prepared for you from the foundation of the world.

For I was an hungred, and ye gave me meat: I was thirsty, and ye gave me drink: I was a stranger, and ye took me in:

Naked, and ye clothed me: I was sick, and ye visited me: I was in prison, and ye came unto me.

Then shall the righteous answer him, saying, Lord, when saw we thee an hungred, and fed thee? or thirsty, and gave thee drink?

When saw we thee a stranger, and took thee in? or naked, and clothed thee?

Or when saw we thee sick, or in prison, and came unto thee?

And the King shall answer and say unto them, Verily I say unto you, inasmuch as ye have done it unto one of the least of these my brethren, ye have done it unto me.

MATTHEW 25:34–40 KJV

These two important passages make it clearer to us what God's cause is. It clearly has something to do with caring for others. If we do not care for or about others, then no amount of churchgoing, no number of observances, no amount of money given, *no amount of believing*, will give us any cause worth working for. In fact, one cannot believe in God in a religious sense unless one has this concern for others.

Now we may be shy or reserved and lacking in confidence, so that we cannot show love easily. We may feel indeed that we are being insincere if we try to do so. We may love Christ truly and deeply, yet be austere by nature. Then let us accept ourselves as we are. It is not reserve but indifference, it is not shyness but coldness, that is the offence against love. Let us heed the advice: "Be yourself. Especially, do not feign affection. Neither be cynical about love; for in the face of all aridity and disenchantment it is perennial as the grass" (from "Desiderata," by Max Ehrmann).

It seems clear that the greatest offence is to be unloving. But love is not primarily giving expression to those tender feelings that are to be found in most human natures. It is primarily consenting to an orderliness of life and to a conscription of one's energy and talents. Love is not a sentimental thing, though I have known people calling themselves Christians to disparage it as such. To me most of these people are afraid of love because they are afraid it might destroy their world.

To love means to bring one's whole life under discipline, extreme in the case of Francis, "wholesome" in the case of most others. This discipline, even if not extreme, means, negatively, refraining from any unloving or mean or cruel act, and positively, the offering of oneself to be made an instrument of God's peace.

⌣⌐ It is the time of the Inquisition, and suddenly Christ is seen in the streets. He is recognised and brought to the Grand Inquisitor, who throws Him into prison, intending to kill Him also. The Grand Inquisitor speaks to Him:

"I too prized the freedom with which Thou hast blessed men, and I too was striving to stand among Thy elect. . . . But I awakened and would not serve madness. I turned back and joined the ranks of those who have corrected Thy work. . . . I repeat, tomorrow Thou shalt see that obedient flock who at a sign from me will hasten to heap up the hot cinders about the pile on which I shall burn Thee for coming to hinder us. For if anyone ever deserved our fires, it is Thou."

When the Inquisitor ceased speaking he waited some time for his Prisoner to answer him. His silence weighed down upon him. He saw that the Prisoner had listened intently all the time, looking gently in his face and evidently not wishing to reply. The old man longed for Him to say something, however bitter and terrible. But he suddenly approached the old man in silence and softly kissed him on his bloodless, aged lips. That was all his answer. The old man shuddered. His lips moved. He went to the door, opened it, and said to him, "Go, and come no more . . . come not at all, never, never." And he let him out into the dark alleys of the town.

DOSTOEVSKY'S THE BROTHERS KARAMAZOV

What does this story mean? It means for one thing that the Church had become an end in itself, and in the name of Christ would break all the commandments of

Christ, using the argument no doubt that if the Church was not preserved, faith would die.

The story has a second meaning, not that Christ showed love to the Grand Inquisitor and so was released, but that Christ's manifestation of love was unendurable. In this story, love is not tenderness, it is judgment.

This is what others have told us about the nature of love:

ST. TERESA: Let everyone understand that real love of God does not consist in tear-shedding, nor in that sweetness and tenderness for which usually we long, just because they console us, but in serving God in justice, fortitude of soul, and humility.

WILLIAM LAW: By love I do not mean any natural tenderness, which is more or less in people according to their constitution; but I mean a larger principle of the soul, founded in reason and piety, which makes us tender, kind, and gentle to all our fellow-creatures as creatures of God, and for his sake.

AN ANECDOTE (which gives yet another manner of regarding love): Dick Sheppard, the beloved, tempestuous, and eccentric vicar of St. Martin-in-the-Fields, was asked by a friend how he could possibly love a certain person, to which Sheppard replied, "I do more than love him, I positively like him!"

O Blessed Jesus, who knowest the impurity of our affection, the narrowness of our sympathy, and the coldness of our love, take possession of our souls and fill our minds with the image of Thyself; break the stubbornness of our selfish wills and mould us in the likeness of Thine unchanging love, O Thou who only could, our Saviour, our Lord and our God. WILLIAM TEMPLE

O Lord, help me to order my life better, help me to use my gifts more industriously, help me to turn from no one in need, help me to see You in the hungry, the sick, the prisoners, the lonely, help me this coming day to do some work of peace for You.

12

Ye are the light of the world.

MATTHEW 5:14 KJV

I came not to judge the world, but to save the world.
JOHN 12:47 KJV

Because ye are not of the world, but I have chosen you out of the world, therefore the world hateth you.
JOHN 15:19 KJV

I pray not that thou shouldest take them out of the world, but that thou shouldest keep them from the evil.
JOHN 17:15 KJV

Love not the world, neither the things that are in the world.   1 JOHN 2:15 KJV

For God so loved the world ... JOHN 3:16 KJV

These passages are confusing, especially to those who look to the Bible for guidance as to their conduct in every possible situation. In some passages the world is the place to be lived in, to be redeemed, to be illumined. In other passages the world is irredeemable, the natural enemy of goodness and faith, a place not to be loved.

Some Christians, mostly members of sects, carry their shunning of the world to extreme lengths. In one of these sects, a man who is converted may no longer have any meaningful commerce with his wife if she is not converted. If a son or daughter will not be converted by a certain age, he or she must be put out of the home. And what is more, a text can be found for it: "I am come to set a man against his father, and the daughter against her mother, and the daughter-in-law against her mother-in-law."

What I hope to do here is to put down the thoughts of a Christian of no rigid belief, who nevertheless has all through his life pondered over these matters, who was brought up by parents who very much wanted their children to keep themselves unspoiled from the world. Alcohol was almost never seen in our home. My father smoked but not my mother, but of course only a small percentage of the women of her generation smoked at all. We played card games, but never for money. We did not dance, go to the racecourse, or play games on Sunday. We went to the cinema but not to the theatre! We were taught a rigid theology, and though it was important both to *believe* and to *do* it was more important to *believe*. In later years I caused my mother much anxiety by saying that if a person tried to lead a good and helpful life, I did not much care what he believed.

We were taught a strict obedience, both to God and to our parents. One of the things that irked us most was that in childhood we were not allowed to go out of the house without supervision, unless to school or on some errand. Later this was relaxed, but our friends had to be approved, and were in large part selected by my father.

Though we rebelled against many of those restrictions, we also learned to love the good, to be dutiful, to help those in need, to hate war and violence. When I went to college I discovered that others had learned the same, with quite a different theology. From that time forward I would have nothing more to do with any rigid system of belief. I married an Anglican girl, and was attracted to Anglicanism because of its "wholesome discipline." I became an Anglican, having shut my eyes and gritted my teeth and swallowed the Thirty-nine Articles. Today racegoing or drinking alcohol or going to the theatre have no relevance to my idea of sin. One of my best friends is a racegoing woman who has the same hopes for South Africa as I do, and is not afraid to expose injustice when she finds it. Today the worst sins to me are cruelty and coldness. Cowardice is no doubt contemptible, but cruelty is horrible. And to me the most horrible form of cruelty is that which men practise in order that some noble end may be achieved.

I have no higher vision of the Church than as the Servant of the World, not withdrawn but participating, not embattled but battling, not condemning but healing the wounds of the hurt and the lost and the lonely, not preoccupied with its survival or its observances or its Articles, but with the needs of mankind.

Now this is often called the social gospel, the turning of the Church into some kind of social welfare society, the exalting of the second commandment over what Jesus called "the first and great commandment." I think I can say something about this. During the Second World War, a wave of idealism surged through the South African armed forces in North Africa and Egypt, a determination to rid South Africa of those gross inequalities of status, wealth and opportunity, that so disfigure our society. This idealism had its counterpart at home, and one consequence of it was the appointment of a commission by Geoffrey Clayton, the great Bishop of Johannesburg, to re-examine the state of our society, and to make recommendations as to the kind of action the Church and Christians should take. The report of the Commission was presented to Synod, and Clayton, who, as chairman, could never conceal his impatience, grew more and more restless as the discussion went on. At last he could bear it no longer, and he jumped to his feet, obviously under the influence of great emotion, and emotion was something he was extremely suspicious of. His voice, always powerful, was now tremendous. "The Church," he said (as I recall), "is not here primarily to serve society. Its prime duty is to worship God and obey Him. And if it is God's will that we should serve society in this or that way, then it is our duty to do it. Let us therefore be very careful that it is God's will we are trying to obey, and that we are not merely trying to make the Church do something that we want to be done. And let me make it quite clear that I appointed this Commission because I believed it might be God's will that we should serve our society in this and that way." Then with a half-embarrassed, half-triumphant look, he ordered that discussion should proceed.

I have only one word to add to this, especially directed to those who do not have the sense of God's being and majesty that was so strong in Bishop Clayton, so strong that it was one of the few things that could evoke in him such emotion. If you do not have this sense, but wish to serve your society and your world, if you wish your life to be used for some purpose, then let your life be used and do not worry unduly about not having this sense. For some people, faith is preliminary to action; for others, action gives reality to faith; in most of us, sometimes one comes first, sometimes the other. I have no doubt that Francis kissed the leper because some tremendous faith was being born in him, and that his faith was tremendously deepened by his act. In our own humble ways, may it be so with us.

Here is thy footstool and there rest thy feet where live the poorest, and lowliest, and lost.

When I try to bow to thee, my obeisance cannot reach down to the depth where thy feet rest among the poorest, and lowliest, and lost.

Pride can never approach to where thou walkest in the clothes of the humble among the poorest, and lowliest, and lost.

My heart can never find its way to where thou keepest company with the companionless among the poorest, the lowliest, and the lost.

TAGORE (who was not a Christian)

Lord, let me not live to be useless.   JOHN WESLEY

13

And one of the Pharisees desired him that he would eat with him. And he went into the Pharisee's house, and sat down to meat.

And, behold, a woman in the city, which was a sinner, when she knew that Jesus sat at meat in the Pharisee's house, brought an alabaster box of ointment.

And stood at his feet behind him weeping, and began to wash his feet with tears, and did wipe them with the hairs of her head, and kissed his feet, and anointed them with the ointment.

Now when the Pharisee which had bidden him saw it, he spoke within himself, saying, This man, if he were a prophet, would have known who and what manner of woman this is that toucheth him: for she is a sinner.

And Jesus answering said unto him, Simon, I have somewhat to say unto thee. And he saith, Master, say on.

There was a certain creditor which had two debtors: the one owed five hundred pence, and the other fifty.

And when they had nothing to pay, he frankly forgave them both. Tell me therefore, which of them will love him most?

Simon answered and said, I suppose that he, to whom he forgave most. And he said unto him, Thou hast rightly judged.

*And he turned to the woman and said unto Simon,
Seest thou this woman? I entered into thine house, thou
gavest me no water for my feet: but she hath washed my
feet with tears, and wiped them with the hairs of her
head.*

*Thou gavest me no kiss: but this woman since the
time I came in hath not ceased to kiss my feet.*

*My head with oil thou didst not anoint: but this
woman hath anointed my feet with ointment.*

*Wherefore I say unto thee, Her sins, which are
many, are forgiven; for she loved much: but to whom
little is forgiven, the same loveth little.*

And he said unto her, Thy sins are forgiven.

*And they that sat at meat with him began to say
within themselves, who is this that forgiveth sins
also?*

*And he said to the woman, Thy faith hath saved
thee; go in peace.*   LUKE 7:36–50 KJV

1

There are several meanings to this story, but one
is very clear—Simon judged and Jesus forgave. Simon
was no doubt an upright man, strict in observance, and
very likely rich. We are not told what he thought of the
coming of this woman uninvited into his house. But we
are told that when the woman washed the feet of Jesus
with her tears, and kissed and anointed them, the first
thought of Simon's was not of the ineffability of the
scene that he was witnessing. His first thought was that
Jesus, for all his reputations, did not know what kind of
woman it was who was touching him.

There is much of Simon in many of us who call ourselves Christians. When we are confronted by sinners (other than ourselves I mean), we are often more inclined to judge than to forgive, we are often more inclined to draw back than to go forward. Some kind of pride inhibits us, possibly some kind of fear. We do not wish to be seen associating with such persons.

When the sinner is repentant, such drawing back is unforgivable. The act of drawing back is then a far greater sin than the one that we are asked to forgive. The word *unforgiving* is one of the nastiest adjectives in the English language.

Love made me welcome: yet my soul drew back,
Guilty of lust and sin.
But quick-eyed love, observing me grow slack
From my first entrance in,
Drew nearer to me, sweetly questioning
If I lacked anything.

A guest, I answered, worthy to be here:
Love said, you shall be he.
I, the unkind, ungrateful? Ah my dear,
I cannot look on thee.
Love took my hand and smiling did reply,
Who made the eyes but I?

Truth Lord, but I have marred them: let my shame
Go where it doth deserve.
And know you not, saith love, who bore the blame?
My dear, then I will serve.
You must sit down, saith love, and taste my meat.
So I did sit and eat.

GEORGE HERBERT

The pride, the strictness, the lack of understanding of Simon the Pharisee, when they are found in us, not only create a vast gulf between ourselves and "sinners,"- but have in our time created a gulf between the old and the young. Older Christians are often repelled by the attitudes of the young towards sex, towards drugs, towards work. Alienation of another kind takes place when older Christians hold firm ideas about patriotism, loyalty, and fighting for one's country. Many young people reject war and violence, and they reject the world that cannot conduct its affairs without the use of war and violence. There is no doubt that many of them would refuse to take part if their country went to war. In my young days it required courage of a very high order to be a conscientious objector in times of war. Chairmen of tribunals could use almost any kind of insulting language to men asking to be exempted from war service. It was taken for granted that they were cowards. That is not the case today amongst the young.

It is often a matter of the utmost difficulty for older Christians to feel love for young people who appear to have rejected all the values of their elders, *and who are unrepentant about it.* Yet to some of these young people, Jesus is a hero. If only he were here now, many of them would flock to him. Have they in their disillusionment and lostness and anger at the world, not retained something of the gospel that we have lost, the knowledge that we must love one another? And when they came to him, would they not see him, not through a haze of marijuana darkly, but face to face, the brother whom they had lost and now had found again?

A Hasidic Story: A father complained to the Baalshem that his son had forgotten God. "What, Rabbi, shall I do?" "Love him more than ever," was the Baalshem's reply.

O Lord teach us to humble ourselves before these children who live the gospel of love and drugs because we did not live the gospel of love. Teach us to humble ourselves before the problems that face our children in this generation. Especially we pray for all parents, that they may love their children steadfastly, even in the face of bewilderment and grief. Teach us to humble ourselves when we contemplate the world we have made, and the millions that we have killed and maimed in causes we believed to be just.

Above all make us the instruments of Your love, so that even if we cannot help them we shall still love them.

This we ask in the name of God who so loved the world, and of his son Jesus, the lover of our souls.

14

Adapt yourselves no longer to the pattern of this present world, but let your minds be remade and your whole nature thus transformed. Then you will be able to discern the will of God, and to know what is good, acceptable, and perfect. PAUL TO THE ROMANS 12:2 NEB

It is one of the good signs of our times that there is such self-criticism within the Church. This self-criticism is practised by both clergy and laity. It is very different from the criticism of those who are outside the Church, and would not particularly want the Church to succeed in practising what it preaches. Nor is it the same as the criticism of those who are members of the Church, who perpetually criticise the Church and especially the clergy because it is their scapegoat for their own failures.

I mean the criticism of those who are fully in the Church, who are distressed by the way it often adapts itself to the "pattern of this present world," who want to see it a witness for Christ in the world. The trouble with witnessing for Christ in the world is that it is at times almost impossible not to antagonise the rich, the well-established, the ruling classes, and important people within the Church itself. If a priest or minister does so, he is stigmatised as a "political parson." Instead of sticking to his work of saving souls, he is "dragging politics into religion." By challenging the "pattern of this present world," he is undermining law and order, and is ignoring Paul's advice to the Romans:

~ Every person must submit to the supreme authorities. There is no authority but by act of God, and the existing authorities are instituted by him; consequently anyone who rebels against authority is resisting a divine institution, and those who so resist have themselves to thank for the punishment they will receive. For government, a terror to crime, has no terrors for good behaviour. You wish to have no fear of the authorities? Then continue to do right and you will have their approval, for they are God's agents working for your good. But if you are doing wrong, then you will have a cause to fear them; it is not for nothing that they hold the power of the sword, for they are God's agents of punishment, for retribution on the offender. That is why you are obliged to submit. It is an obligation imposed not merely by fear of retribution but by conscience. That is also why you pay taxes. The authorities are in God's service and to these duties they devote their energies.   *Romans 13:1–6* NEB

I am one of those Christians who find it impossible to reconcile Romans, chapter 12, verse 2, and Romans, chapter 13, verses 1–6. In this second passage St. Paul seems to suggest that the "existing authorities" are the guardians of morality, and that if we do right, we need not fear the authorities. St. Paul's life and death were irrefutable proofs that this is not true. Jesus was crucified by the "existing authorities" who were "God's agents." Nothing in the teachings of Jesus suggests that to follow him will ensure a quiet life, acceptable to the powers that be. I myself have friends of what is called "unimpeachable character" who are restricted in movement and are not allowed to attend any social gathering because they did not adapt themselves to the pattern of their present world.

When Peter and others had angered the High Priest by their teaching, they were brought before the Sanhedrin:

"We expressly ordered you," the High Priest said, "to desist from teaching in that name; and what has happened? You have filled Jerusalem with your teaching, and you are trying to make us responsible for that man's death." Peter replied for himself and the apostles: "We must obey God rather than man." (Acts 5:28-29 NEB)

The belief that the Church must never challenge the State, except in extreme cases which seldom arise, is deeply rooted in many parts of the Church. The belief that the Church must challenge the State if the State embarks on any action which runs counter to Christ's teaching, is also deeply rooted. This leads to compromises, not only within the Church but between Church and State.

WILLIAM TEMPLE: One of the commonest of the compromises that have been made is for the world to allow the Church to be at peace in proclaiming what may be called its philosophical paradoxes provided that it keeps quiet about its moral ones.

Not for one moment must we underestimate the immense problem of the coexistence of Church and State, nor the problem of how to follow the teachings of Jesus in a secular society. It is no answer to say we must be more loving. Francis faced the same problem. While on a preaching mission in the foothills of the Apennines, he heard that there was to be a tournament at Montefeltro Castle. Although he had left the pleasures of the world, he decided to go to the tournament, and mingled happily with the gay crowd. At some point he climbed on to some seat or pillar and asked for silence so that he might speak. Then he preached to them of the heavenly country, touching their hearts. When he had finished, one of the great nobles, Lord Orlando dei Cattani, asked if they could speak together, and Francis agreed willingly to do so when the noble lord had done his social duties. And what did Lord Orlando ask him? Something that we might have asked him too, for he wanted to know not how to join the Order, but how to live the Christian life in the world. And when Francis said he would help him, Orlando asked him to accept a gift for his Order, which was nothing less than the mountain of Alvernia in the Apennines, where Francis later received the five wounds.

Thus was born at Montefeltro the Third Order, for those who had lives to live and duties to do in the world. Christians in the world had first to love God, to praise Him, to practise prayer, and be obedient to God's commandments. They were to love their neighbours as themselves, and to be the servants of all, remembering especially the poor. They were to accord justice to all and to practise mercy. They were to be charitable to their enemies, honest in business, moderate in the use of food and drink and clothes, disciplined in life, and self-denying. They were to be loyal to the Church, observing its rites, taking part in its fasts and its feasts, especially the Blessed Sacrament, repenting them of their sins, and receiving God with a pure heart and chaste body.

Francis wrote all these things down in his "Letter to All Christians," and this letter formed the basis of the Rule of the Third Order. Such a man as Lord Orlando, who was one of the first to be admitted, continued to administer his estates as before, but with a new hope and aim. Rich merchants eschewed luxury. The Third Order was the answer to many who needed guidance as to how to live in the world without conforming to the accepted pattern of things.

An Addendum (the author greatly daring): There is no such thing as *saving souls*, unless we save them for something. We cannot save them for God, because they are his already. But we may save them for some purpose of God. We may save them by inspiring them, not to belong to God which they do already, but to become his instruments, thus making themselves part of the Divine Creativity that rules the world. If a soul makes itself part of that, then it is saved. A Christian may believe, as we have seen earlier, that certain of our social arrangements are such as to make it almost impossible for a man to conceive himself as part of the Divine Creativity, or to take part in his work, which means, of course, that he cannot realise himself as a man. If a Christian wishes to work for the removal of such impediments, then he is not bringing politics into religion, he is trying to save souls for the purpose for which they were created.

NICHOLAS BERDYAEV: The present state of the world calls for a moral and spiritual revolution, revolution in the name of personality, of men, of every single person. This revolution should restore the hierarchy of values, now quite shattered, and place the value of human personality above the idols of production, technics, the State, race, nationality, the collective.

❧ O God, . . . teach us to live together in love and joy and peace; to check all bitterness; to disown discouragement; to practice thanksgiving, and to leap with joy to any task for others. Strengthen the good thing thus begun; that with gallant and high-hearted happiness we may work for thy Kingdom in the wills of men. Through Jesus Christ our Lord. THE PRAYER OF TOC H.

God grant me the serenity to accept the things I cannot change, courage to change the things I can, and the wisdom to know the difference. REINHOLD NIEBUHR

O Lord, grant that we may not be conformed to the world, but may love it and serve it. Grant we may never shrink from being the instruments of Thy peace because of the judgment of the world. Grant that we may love Thee without fear of the world, grant that we may never believe that the inexpressible majesty of Thyself may be found in any power of this earth. May we firstly love Thee and our neighbours as ourselves. May we remember the poor and the prisoner and the sick and the lonely, and the young searchers, and the tramps and vagabonds, and the lost and the lonely, as we remember Christ, who is in them all. And may we this coming day be able to do some work of peace for Thee.

15

Where there is sorrow, let me bring joy; where there is darkness, light.

PRAYER OF ST. FRANCIS

A university president from the United States was on a visit to South Africa, and he made a special point of visiting with me. When he returned to America he wrote to me telling me that I was not the kind of person he had expected to see. I replied asking him what he meant, and he wrote back that he had expected to see me more a man of joy, and what he meant was, a man of Christian joy.

This observation, which was as sharp and clean as a knife, led me to do some thinking, and although I did not wish to obtrude myself unduly in this book, I cannot escape it now.

Why can I not be described as joyful? Why on the whole can my friends not be described as joyful? Most of them have a decided sense of humour, and all of them have experienced joyful occasions, reunions, blessings, achievements, and expect to experience many more. People have been known to shout for joy, leap for joy, dance for joy, weep for joy. All these things they do *on joyous occa-*

sions. Some of the most spectacular joyous occasions are those on which our cause has triumphed, and someone else's cause has been defeated!

These joyous occasions I understand well. I have often experienced them. I have often been able to be the bringer of joy to others; this is a country in which small things, small gifts, small recognitions, small identifications, can bring disproportionate joy. Not only does one bring joy, one experiences joy in bringing it. And the reason is that when one brings joy, and when one experiences joy in bringing it, one has what I can only describe as an experience of God. I am not speaking of mystical experience, because I do not have much mystical experience. What I am speaking of, to coin a pretty terrible phrase, is the joy of instrumentality. The more I am used as an instrument, the closer do I approach a state of abiding joy.

The world, however, is a tough place. It brings frustrations, and frustrations in this context mean that one's instrumentality is restricted in its scope by forces that one does not control. This calls for fortitude, patience, and constancy. These are the qualities of the friends with whom I have worked. Not for a moment do I suppose that they are the only ones who have them, nor do I suppose that those who are opposed to me do not have them.

Now I think it is quite possible that the espousal of a cause which one believes to be worthy of one's devotion, the facing of difficulties with fortitude, patience, and constancy, the willingness to endure suffering for the sake of this cause, can bring joy. Instantly there comes to my mind the famous photograph of Gandhi and Nehru sitting together on a mat, with Gandhi the picture of childlike gaiety, which is a manifestation of joy. That Jesus could be gay, I could not for a moment question, though the Gospels do not tell us about it; they tell us much more about the graver joy of a hard course chosen and pursued to the end.

Therefore, while I wish I could be more joyous, and do more of this shouting, leaping, dancing, and weeping, I shall tell myself to accept myself, which as everyone knows, is dangerous advice. I shall not take too desperate a view of my own situation. I remember, though not well, one of the well-known stories of World War II, told of the man who was responsible for the safety of British merchant shipping. This man I shall call Sir John, but that was probably not his name. Things were going pretty badly for British shipping, and one of Sir John's colleagues was in his office, filling the air with gloom. Sir John said to him sharply, "You've forgotten Rule No. 4." His colleague asked with surprise, "What's Rule No. 4?" "Rule No. 4," said Sir John, "is 'Don't take yourself too seriously.'" His colleague asked, "What are the other rules?" Sir John replied, "There aren't any others." So I shall try, and those like me should try, too, not to take too serious a view of our failure to attain this state of permanent joy. St. Francis did it, but, as someone said to me reproachfully, "St. Francis was a saint!" Yet he, too, passed through a long period of what could only be called absence of joy.

This year a friend of mine wished me a happy Easter, and I, because my wife was gravely ill, replied that I did not think it would be happy. When he reached home, he sat down and wrote to me that no Christian should be unhappy at Easter because what had happened at Easter was of an eternal order, whereas our griefs were temporal.

I replied to him that I did not expect to be unhappy

at Easter. I was prepared to face the future and whatever it might bring. I wrote: "I like to see happiness and to see happy people, especially happy children. I hope they may grow up happy also, but if I had to choose, I would rather see them brave."

And many of those I know have had to choose. They do not show the outward signs of joy, but they have an inner fortitude, a kind of inner equilibrium that has cost too much to be tranquility, and is still too much on guard to be serenity. I think that such an inner equilibrium might possibly be called joy.

Suppose that one experienced a deep personal grief, just at Eastertime. Could one be happy as well? I try not to think in these categories at all. The grief will go, the deeper fortitude will stay. And this fortitude comes from the faith that the things we believe in and the things we try to do are right.

Make me, O Lord, the instrument of Thy love, that I may bring comfort to those who sorrow and joy to those who are regarded as persons of little account. In this country of many races make me courteous to those who are humble and understanding to those who are resentful. Teach me what I should be to the arrogant and cruel, for I do not know.

And as for me myself, make me more joyful than I am, especially if this is needed for the sake of others. Let me remember my many experiences of joy and thankfulness, especially those that endure. And may I this coming day do some work of peace for Thee.

16

O Divine Master, grant that I may not so much seek to be consoled, as to console; not so much to be understood, as to understand; not so much to be loved, as to love.

PRAYER OF ST. FRANCIS

It is about seventeen years since I first read the prayer which is the subject of these meditations. Why I had never seen it before, I do not know. Since that time I have met more and more people who know it, and who find that it speaks to them firmly and clearly in these shifting times. I suppose it would be true to say that no religion in the world has become so entangled with dogma and doctrine and creed as has our own. The great commandments are two. The first is to love God with heart and soul and mind; the second is to love our neighbours as ourselves. *On these two commandments hang all the law and the prophets.* And let us remember, there are many people who have been led to understand and obey the first commandment because they tried to be obedient to the second.

ST. TERESA: We cannot know whether we love God, although there may be strong reasons for thinking so, but there can be no doubt about whether we love our neighbour or no. Be sure that in proportion as you advance in fraternal charity, you are increasing in your love of God, for His Majesty bears so tender an affection for us, that I cannot doubt He will repay our love for others by augmenting, in a thousand different ways, that which we bear for Him.

What more encouraging words could there be than these, especially for those who love the Good, and are searching for the God from whom all Good comes? What encouragement to be told by a saint that we cannot know whether we love God, although there may be strong reasons for thinking so! I am attracted to many people who love the Good and live their lives as though under some obedience; and I find that they in their turn are attracted to those Christians who try to obey the two great commandments. Whatever else shifts, these two do not shift. On them all else is built—morality, theology, ideals, principles. Yet nothing that is built on them must ever supersede them. If they are ever superseded, then we get that loveless Christianity that is more concerned with law, authority, abstentions, and observances, than with the prisoner in the prison house. I know this Christianity, I have sat in councils with it, its face is too terrible to look upon. No wonder Jesus had such a love for sinners.

The first petition of St. Francis, that he should be the instrument of God's peace, is the greatest that any Christian can offer, and it is followed by six subpetitions, each of them elements of the first, each sublime in its intention. And no sooner have we been overwhelmed by it than it is followed by a second petition of equal power, that one should seek not so much to be consoled as to console, a petition offered with a purity and a humility which move me as deeply as I write now as ever they did before. Yet Francis does not say that he does not wish to be consoled, understood, and loved. He is willing to receive, for if he is not willing to receive, then he is preventing someone from giving.

That is what Peter once tried to do; he tried to prevent someone from giving.

During supper, Jesus, well aware that the Father had entrusted everything to him, and that he had come from God and was going back to God, rose from table, laid aside his garments, and taking a towel, tied it round him. Then he poured water into a basin, and began to wash his disciples' feet and to wipe them with the towel.

When it was Simon Peter's turn, Peter said to him, "You, Lord, washing my feet?" Jesus replied, "You do not understand now what I am doing, but one day you will." Peter said, "I will never let you wash my feet." "If I do not wash you," Jesus replied, "you are not in fellowship with me." "Then, Lord," said Simon Peter, "not my feet only; wash my hands and head as well." . . .

After washing their feet and taking his garments again, he sat down. "Do you understand," he asked, "what I have done for you? You call me 'Master' and 'Lord,' and rightly so, for that is what I am. Then if I, your Lord and Master, have washed your feet, you also ought to wash one another's feet. I have set you an example; you are to do as I have done for you. In very truth I tell you, a servant is not greater than his master, nor a messenger than the one who sent him. If you know this, happy are you if you act upon it." *John 13* NEB

In my own country, where there are many races, and where race difference is established and maintained by law, it is difficult for many members of the so-called superior groups to serve those of the so-called inferior groups. For every white man who would help an old black woman to cross a busy street, there would be some who would not; though perhaps some of those would wish that they *could* do so. But once the barrier is crossed, the whole personality becomes richer and gentler. There is only one way in which man's inhumanity to man can be made endurable to us, and that is when we in our own lives try to exemplify man's humanity to man.

It sometimes happens in this country that a poor person brings a gift to one not poor. If it is done in love and kindness or gratitude, then it should be received. Let us seek not so much to be consoled as to console, but when it is our turn to be consoled, then let us receive such consolation with humility and thanks.

Teach us, good Lord, to serve Thee as Thou deservest; to give and not to count the cost; to fight and not to heed the wounds; to toil and not to ask for rest; to labour and not to ask for any reward, save that of knowing that we do Thy will. Through Jesus Christ our Lord.

ST. IGNATIUS OF LOYOLA

17

Racial warfare flared in Detroit agàin yesterday, and the death toll rose to 35. There had been a few hours of calm —during which Black leaders threatened guerilla warfare and said: "We stand on the eve of a Black revolution."

Violence also flared in another seven Michigan cities yesterday—Saginaw, Grand Rapids, Pontiac, Flint, Muskegon, Benton Harbor and Mount Clemens.

THE NATAL MERCURY (MORNING EDITION)
JULY 27, 1967

2000 crack American paratroopers, some just back from Vietnam, are still guarding East Detroit.

Rioting continued last night in Toledo, Cincinnati, Chicago, Cambridge (Maryland), San Francisco and Phoenix. At least 20 people were arrested in Toledo after Negroes had thrown fire bombs and looted shops.

THE DAILY NEWS (EVENING EDITION)
JULY 27, 1967

Tired Federal troops finally curbed America's costliest-ever riots in Detroit yesterday, but more Negro violence exploded in other cities across the country.

In Los Angeles, fire-bombs were thrown in the streets of the Watts section—a grim reminder of the six-day 1965 riots there in which 35 people died.

Guardsmen used riot gas in Cambridge, Maryland, to disperse 400 Negroes who had gathered for a street rally. The town was the scene of a violent riot two days ago. THE NATAL MERCURY, JULY 28, 1967

Stokely Carmichael has issued from Havana a threat of Black vengeance. . . . "We are not waiting for them to kill us. We will move to kill them first, or rather, we are working towards that goal. . . . One good thing about the Vietnam war is that the United States has taught us how to kill. Our brothers returning from Vietnam are going to use that training well in the cities of the United States."

THE NATAL MERCURY, AUGUST 3, 1967

When I read this news my heart aches, not only for America but for myself too. Why is there all this depth of hatred, and when did it begin? It had several sources and slavery is certainly one of them. In the fifteenth, sixteenth, seventeenth, eighteenth, and even nineteenth centuries after Christ, the ships of Europe carried slaves from Africa to the New World. In 1790, according to the *Encyclopaedia Britannica*, 74,000 Africans were forcibly removed from the west coast of Africa. Of these one-eighth would die on the journey, one-twentieth die in the harbour, and one-third die in the "seasoning." It is estimated by some that twenty million Africans were abducted from Africa during the life of the trade. Some fell into the hands of humane masters, some lived lives of unspeakable misery, suffering the extremes of cruelty and degradation. All lived the lives of slaves.

ABRAHAM LINCOLN (in his Second Inaugural): Fondly do we hope—fervently do we pray—that this mighty scourge of war may speedily pass away. Yet, if God wills that it continue, until all the wealth piled by the bond-man's two hundred and fifty years of unrequited toil shall be sunk, and until every drop of blood drawn with the lash shall be paid for by another drawn with the sword, as it was said three thousand years ago, so still it must be said, "the judgments of the Lord are true and righteous altogether."

Lincoln certainly would have called these riots judgments of the Lord. The harvest we are reaping comes from the seed that we have sowed. What must be done now? Clearly the main task falls to the authorities, to create that kind of society in which hatred will die away, because when there is hope, purpose, recognition, then hatred does die away. This society has been called the Great Society, but no great society will ever be built as long as there exist gross inequalities of income, opportunity, and status. To remove these is going to cost a lot of money, a lot of thought, a lot of work. We shall never build the Great Society so long as we pour our money into armaments. And what is hardest of all, we shall have to endure hatred while we are building it. While we are building it we are going to be hated, cursed, stoned, shot at, perhaps even killed, by some of the very people for whom we are building it. We are going to have to go on building while we are being hated. I doubt whether any nation has ever before been faced with such a task.

But it has to be undertaken. The alternatives are unthinkable. One alternative would be to partition the United States of America. The other would be to go back to segregation, to the shooting, lynching, hanging, back to real segregation, with stockades, gates, barbed wire, floodlights, armed guards, machine guns, death rays, and if that doesn't solve the problem, back to the gas chambers. America cannot go back one inch on that road. So great is the crisis confronting her that she would be justified in organising a great army, not to fight the enemies abroad but those at home, using all the energy and idealism of her young people, many of whom would willingly devote their lives to such a cause, many of whom are now rebels without any cause at all.

When I face some problem whose solution seems impossible, I always think of London on October 15, 1940, when 480 German aircraft dropped an estimated 386 tons of high explosive and 70,000 incendiary bombs. The incendiary bombs were something new, and while Londoners sheltered in the basements, strategic and historic buildings burned out above their heads. If this were to go on night after night, nothing of London would be left. And what could Londoners possibly do? " 'To the basements,' " wrote Churchill, "must be replaced by 'To the roofs.' " What had seemed a hopeless future became an inspiring present. Everyone pressed forward to do his or her share. "Many became adept," wrote Churchill, "and thousands of fires were extinguished before they took hold. The experience of remaining on the roof night after night under fire, with no protection but a tin hat, soon became habitual."

What Londoners did then, we must do now, because people are threatening to "burn America down."

And what must *I* do, apart from what I do as a citizen enrolled by my government at a time of national crisis, or as a member of some civic or church or other group? I must try to understand what makes people hate, loot, and kill. If I am white, then I must try to understand the consequences of that amazing intellectual flowering of the West, accompanied by technological advances that enabled the people and nations of Europe to go into every country of the world, and virtually to do what they liked, even to the extent of annexing whole countries that belonged to other people, that tremendous historical process known as colonisation, which was as catastrophic in its undoing as it was in its doing, so catastrophic that it will take the world generations to recover from it all. If I am tempted to point to African wars, I must remember World War I and World War II, and the massacre of the Jews by Hitler. If I am tempted to sneer at Congo chaos, then I must remember who prepared the way for it. If I am angered by Congo brutality, then let me also remember Leopold II. If I am tempted to hate, and if I fall to the temptation, then either I repent, or I cease to be a Christian.

There is only one thing I can do in times like these, when some people, and some of them very intelligent people, fear a total estrangement between black and white. Then I, whether I am black or white, must ask to be made an instrument of God's peace, so that one more healing stream may flow into the river of hate. It is hard for me to see God's power working in these dangerous times, unless it works through us.

In April, 1958, when Dag Hammarskjold was beginning his second term, the Staff gave him a surprise party, and he made a speech of thanks. He concluded, Henry P. Van Dusen tells us, with a favourite verse from the Swedish poet Gunnar Ekelöf: "Will the day ever come when joy is great and sorrow small?" and added his own answer: "On the day we feel we are living with a duty, well fulfilled and worth our while, on that day joy is great and we can look on sorrow as being small."

> *Lord, strengthen us in these troublous times. Save us from a retreat into hatred or despair. Call us out of the shelters and send us up to the roofs, even if day and night we are under fire. Help us to rebuild the house that is broken down, and to put out the flames before they destroy us all. Rebuke us for any self-pity, and teach us rather to keep our pity for others who need it. May we remain calm in the midst of violence and panic, and may reason and love and mercy and understanding rule our lives. And may we this coming day be able to do some work of peace for Thee.*

18

For it is in giving that we receive.

PRAYER OF ST. FRANCIS

If you love, you will be loved;
If you respect people, you will be respected;
If you serve them, you will be served;
If you give a good account of yourself toward others, others
*   will act likewise toward you.*
Blessed is the man who loves and does not desire to be
*   loved for it;*
Blessed is he who respects others and does not look for re-
*   spect in return;*
who serves and does not expect service for it; who acquits
*   himself well of others and does not desire that they re-*
*   turn the grace.*
Because such things are big, foolish people do not rise to
*   them.*   BROTHER GILES

No one has ever found a satisfactory explanation of the source of the prayer of St. Francis. The saying of Brother Giles given above is obviously akin to the prayer, and may well have been inspired by it, for Brother Giles joined the Order in 1209, and was a member of it for over fifty years until his death in 1262. This has led some to think that he knew the prayer, and that he knew it because it was composed by St. Francis.

The meaning of the saying is clearly, "It is in giving that we receive, and blessed is he who gives without thought of receiving." I venture to think that St. Francis meant that quite apart from any expectation or lack of it, in giving we *do* receive. We cannot do anything but receive because that is a law of our being. There is only one condition attached to it, and that is that when we give, it must be ourselves that we are giving. The gift, the money, the book, the flowers, are only symbols in this kind of giving, they are signs that it is ourselves that we are giving.

It is not uncommon in a society where there is great disparity of wealth for the "haves" to argue amongst themselves as to whether the "have-nots" are grateful or ungrateful. Some "haves" are obsessed with a belief in the ingratitude of the "have-nots," to the extent that they are embittered by it. "I gave him this and I gave him that, and look what he did to me!" That there are cases of ingratitude one cannot doubt, but apart from those it is my experience that those who complain of ingratitude never give themselves with their gifts. It is the gift, the thing, the money, that they expect to evoke the response, and very often it does not. But when we give ourselves, not seeking gratitude, we are often overwhelmed by the response in some other person who at that moment gives himself to us. It is in that moment that we receive; it is in that moment that God is; it is in that place that God is. That, above all, is what we receive, and it is an experience of joy. And that for me is one of the meanings of God, that He is in that time and place where you and I give of ourselves to each other.

Sometimes it happens that I give myself and you take, but you do not give yourself. This often happens in love between man and woman. Far from bringing joy it brings pain. Sometimes it happens that I give myself and you will not even take. This happened to Jesus, and drew from him the cry, "O Jerusalem, Jerusalem, thou that killest the prophets, and stonest them which are sent unto thee, how often would I have gathereth thy children together, even as a hen gathereth her chickens under her wings, and ye would not!" Yet one cannot read the fourteenth, fifteenth, sixteenth, and seventeenth chapters of St. John's Gospel without realising that in giving greatly, so did Jesus receive. Did he not say: "Give, and it shall be given unto you; good measure, pressed down, and shaken together, and running over, shall men give into your bosom. For with the same measure that ye mete withal it shall be measured to you again."

Luke 6:38 KJV

One of the most tragic characters I have ever met was a priest who had spent the greater part of his life as a missionary in Swaziland, and came to Johannesburg to retire. When I asked him about his life among the Swazis, to my astonishment his mouth began to quiver with pain and his eyes to fill with tears, and he said to me with a mixture of anger and hurt, "I do not like to speak about it; they are the most ungrateful people in the world." Something had gone wrong with the manner of giving.

Compare this with the story of the Curé d'Ars. He was a dunce at school and distressed his parents by deciding to become a priest. So deep was his devotion that the authorities virtually pushed him through the seminary, and in his first parish the vicar thought him too stupid to let him preach. But the Bishop had more insight, and appointed him Curé of Ars. From this small parish his fame slowly spread throughout all France. Hundreds of thousands of people, great and small, made their pilgrimage to Ars, to hear him preach, to touch him, to confess to him, to be absolved, to be blessed. When he left his church to go to his room, so great was the crowd, so urgent their demands, that it took him thirty minutes to cross the square. He was canonised in 1925, some 66 years after his death, and in 1929 was made the patron saint of parish priests. He gave abundantly of what appeared to be the most humble gifts, and received in abundance also. Even the unbelieving world recognised in him the instrument of some supreme Power.

What does giving oneself to God mean? Whatever else it means, it certainly means giving oneself to others.

✠ *Lord, help me to give myself when I am giving. Teach me to give without thought of receiving, and to receive without thought of giving. Teach me not to withhold or to withdraw myself. Teach me to hoard nothing: love, money, time, possessions. Make me ready to give, even my life if it is required of me. And while I have it, use it as an instrument of Your peace.*

19

It is in pardoning that we are pardoned.

PRAYER OF ST. FRANCIS

We have discussed the subject of forgiveness, but not the implication of the petition in the Lord's Prayer, "Forgive us the wrong we have done, as we have forgiven those who have wronged us." Jesus goes on, after the prayer is ended, to say, "For if you forgive others the wrong they have done, your heavenly Father will also forgive you; but if you do not forgive others, then the wrongs you have done will not be forgiven by your Father."

How is this to be interpreted? I know that in trying to interpret I lay myself open to the charge that I interpret things the way I like them to be.

These are my difficulties:

(1) It sounds as if Jesus is saying, "If you do this, then God will do that; but if you don't, he won't either." I find this hard to believe of God—who causes his rain to fall on both the just and the unjust.

(2) When Jesus said, "Father forgive them, for they know not what they do," he seems to imply a forgiveness that is freely given, even to those who have not repented.

(3) It is my reading of "love your enemies and pray for your persecutors" that we are being enjoined to love them and pray for them, even when they have not repented or do not have any intention of repenting. And surely we cannot love them if we have not forgiven them. If this can be expected of us, how may we expect less of God?

Greatly daring, I would venture this interpretation: If you do not forgive those who have wronged you, then your heavenly Father will not be able to forgive you, for you will never be able to recognise forgiveness so long as you have not forgiven these others.

It seems to me that there are at least two kinds of forgiveness. There is one kind in which one person forgives another, but the forgiven person does not know and may not care that he has been forgiven. A son who has caused his mother much grief may at last repent, and ask for forgiveness, and the mother may well reply, "Son, I forgave you long ago." This kind of forgiveness was shown by the father of the prodigal son, who saw his son when he was still a great way off, and ran and fell on his neck and kissed him. Yet even in this first kind of forgiveness, which is very wonderful, the relationship is only restored when, and does not exist until, the second person has repented.

The other kind of forgiveness is that in which the second person first repents and is then forgiven. This frequently happens between husband and wife; the one hurts the other and, after a time when pride has come to its senses, says "I am sorry," and the relationship is immediately restored.

Now it seems to me that God may well forgive us

while we are still a great way off, and perhaps not even on the way home at all. *But for us ourselves it is essential that we ask for forgiveness; otherwise we shall not recognise or experience it.* It is essential that we should have forgiven others, for our relationship with others is one way of knowing God. We cannot hope to be instruments of God's peace when we ourselves are not at peace with others, and certainly not when we hate them.

〜 If, when you are bringing your gift to the altar, you suddenly remember that your brother has a grievance against you, leave your gift where it is before the altar. First go and make your peace with your brother, and only then come back and offer your gift.   *Matthew 5:23* NEB

In a small town near the place where I live, a young married man killed and mutilated a young girl with whom he had been having a love affair. For this he was sentenced to death; and while he was awaiting execution, the parents of the dead girl let it be known through the medium of the newspapers that they had forgiven him. This action was generally considered a noble one, even by those who said that they themselves could never have taken it.

Furthermore it is generally considered churlish in a person if he refuses forgiveness to one who asks for it. I have had this experience. When I was a young schoolmaster, I looked after some seventy boys in one wing of the school hostel, and the senior matron was responsible for about the same number of girls in the other wing. One afternoon when I returned from school, I found that the matron had shut two small girls in a cupboard for some offence or other. In my anger I told her that her action was disgraceful, after which she would not speak to me. The atmosphere in our common dining room was decidedly unpleasant, and when the second matron advised me to apologise, I did so. However, the senior matron refused to accept my apology, and for two long years we ate our meals at the same table and never exchanged a word with each other. In fact she became my enemy. She became actively hostile to anything I did or said. Did I love her? I certainly did not. For me she was the apotheosis of astringent spinsterhood.

I think it is true to say that in South Africa the gulf between white apartheiders and their opponents is wide and deep, as wide and deep a gulf as exists in any country. The differences are political, but moral too. The apartheiders think that their opponents, especially their white ones, are traitors to the country, agitators, communists, or liberals (which is just as bad because liberals in their fatuous sentimentality open the gates for the communists to enter the holy city). The opponents think that many of the policies of apartheid are cruel and indifferent to human suffering, and that many apartheiders know this, but think the ideal of racial separation so noble as to justify such means. What is more, the apartheiders wield tremendous temporal power and their opponents none, and this power is used to ban, banish, silence, and forbid social intercourse to those who are most active in opposition.

Thus the relationship that exists is virtually one of enmity. I just do not know how else to describe it. *I should like to place on record that I do not hate my opponents.* I also must place on record that I do not love them, not in any sense of the word "love" as I know it.

If "love your enemies" means "regard your enemies as children of God, and treat them with humanity," then I would understand it, but it would still be to me an evasion.

I do not quite know why I do not hate my enemies. I know from experience that hate is corrosive, and that one who hates does terrible damage to his own character and personality; but I doubt whether one can refrain from feeling so powerful an emotion just because one has such experiential knowledge. I can only thank God that I am not given to hating. What is more, I thank God for the knowledge that one becomes less and less given to hating as one becomes more and more given to loving.

I close with a last observation. When I read Matthew, chapter 23, I find it hard to believe that Jesus loved the legalists and the Pharisees and the hypocrites. Had one of them come to him seeking, as Nicodemus did, I do not doubt that he would have loved him. If Jesus *did* love the legalists and the Pharisees and the hypocrites, then he loved them in some sense of the word "love" that I do not understand.

James B. Pratt, in *India and Its Faiths*, tells the story of the Indian who, at the time of the Mutiny, greeted the soldier about to bayonet him with the extraordinary words, "And thou too art divine." That this is sublime, who would question? And I read·into it the meaning that the man about to die is in that moment at one with the Divine, so that his love reaches out even to the man who is about to kill him. I conclude that the nearer one is to the Divine, the more one is able to love one's enemies, and that I myself am far from it, though I wish to be nearer.

Lord, teach me the meaning of Your commandment to love our enemies, and help me to obey it. Make me the instrument of Your love, which is not denied to the hungry, the sick, the prisoner, the enemy.

Teach me to hate division, and not to seek after it. But teach me also to stand up for those things that I believe to be right, no matter what the consequences may be.

And help me this day to do some work of peace for You, perhaps to one whom I had thought to be my enemy.

20

It is in dying that we are born to eternal life.

PRAYER OF ST. FRANCIS

What did St. Francis mean by this? Was he speaking of the afterlife, the life after death? The story of his dying relates that he had no fear of death. There was not a thought in his mind that his death meant the end of his relationship with his friend and his Most High Lord. On the contrary it would continue, and it would continue for ever. Yet it was not in this dying that he entered into eternal life; he had done that already, in his first dying, which began when he came down from his horse that day on the Umbrian plain.

It seems to me that in his prayer, St. Francis is speaking of the first kind of dying. When we give, something is given to us. When we pardon, pardon is given to us. So when we die, life is given to us. St. Francis is not speaking of some event not yet come. He is speaking of an event of which he has already had experience, of an event which is continually, perhaps continuously, happening. He is speaking of the kind of life of which Jesus spoke when he said that he had come so that we might have life and have it more abundantly. In other words, he had come so that we might have eternal life.

This view seems confirmed by the last stanza of *Canticle of the Sun,* which he added a few days before his death:

Praised be my Lord for our sister, the bodily death,
From which no living man can flee.
Woe to them who die in mortal sin,
Blessed those who shall find themselves in Thy most holy
    will,
For the second death shall do them no ill.

It is difficult for many Christians to adopt wholly this interpretation of eternal life, because they are preoccupied with what is called the afterlife, the life after death. The view is often held by Christians that if there is no life after death, then life before death has no meaning. This life after death has been described both by those who have had no experience of it, and (so we are told) by those who are actually experiencing it, according to whom it appears to be one of great insipidity. The descriptions of those who have no experience of it are, inevitably so, more imaginative. There seems to be a great deal of singing and praise and music in heaven, according to some. According to others, we take up where we left off. According to yet others, we are reunited with loved ones; this is the comfort given by many priests and ministers to bereaved persons. One of the latest and most imaginative efforts was made very recently by an English Swedenborgian who, in defiance of Jesus' statement that there is no marriage in

116

heaven, asserts that those who have bad marital luck on earth will have good (and new) marital luck in heaven.

I should like to set down here my own belief. In so far as I am willing to be made an instrument of God's peace, in that far have I already entered into eternal life. Heaven to me is here, and whatever else it may be, I can know it now in so far as I am the instrument of that peace. What happens to me after I die, I do not know, nor do I really want to know. I have no evidence on which to deny that there is life after death, but what kind of life it would be, I have no idea. That a man who, in the words of Francis, was in God's will remains in that will, I am prepared to believe, because Francis, when death came, welcomed it; he called death, Sister Death, and said to his doctor, "She is to me the gate of life." So should I like to die.

There are some diffident Christians who cannot believe that they are now in eternal life, not only because they continue to think of eternal life as a reward for this one, but because they think it is far too grand a way to describe the prosaic way in which they live. They feel that such descriptions must be reserved for the saints and perhaps the clergy! Yet the gospel is a gospel for *us*, it is good news for *us*. When Jesus said, "You are the light of the world," he was not speaking to the saints and the clergy, he was speaking to people like *us*. So let us think and reflect more on the proposition that we are even now in eternal life, and whatever happens after the physical death, we do so continue, for we are in God's will, and God's will continues.

Two last points: The dying of the first death is not always a dramatic encounter; sometimes it takes a long time. The second point is that we do not cease to be sinners because we enter into eternal life; both St. Paul and St. Francis claimed to be superlative sinners.

~~ In midsummer of the year 1224 Francis was carried back to Assisi to die. His pains were great and continuous. He was lodged in the Bishop's house, and an armed guard was set about it, in case the people of Perugia would try to take him to their own town.

At first the doctor evaded his questions, but Francis said to him, "I am not a cuckoo to be afraid of death. By the grace of the Holy Spirit I am so intimately united to God that I am equally content to live or die." When the doctor replied that he would die at the end of September or the beginning of October, Francis stretched out his hands and cried aloud with joy, "Welcome, Sister Death." He sent for Angelo and Leo and asked them to sing for him his *Canticle of the Sun,* and after they had sung it he added the stanza "Praised be my Lord for our sister, the bodily death."

From that day to the end there was always singing in his room, in which he joined when he was able. Elias, who was now Minister-General of the Order, did not think this seemly, and he asked Francis to stop it, but for once Francis disobeyed him, declaring that he was rejoicing in the Lord.

When he was near death, the brothers gathered round him asking for his blessing, Elias on his left, and Bernard, his first disciple, on his right. But Francis wished to bless Elias with his right hand, to show him that he knew he was penitent and wished to forgive him. Therefore he crossed his arms so that his right hand was on the head of

Elias, and the crossed arms are now the symbol of the Franciscan Order.

Francis now begged to go home to the Portiuncula, and how could Elias now deny him? Though he was blind he knew when the road reached a point where there was a clear view of Assisi. He asked to be placed facing it, and raising himself and his hand also, blessed the city and its people.

Home at the Portiuncula, he made a strange request. He asked to be well clothed upon his bier, and to have candles about him, and a cushion for his head. He saw no sin in it, because his body would be dead and would feel no pleasure. He dictated a last letter to Lady Clare, beseeching her in no wise to depart from the holy life and from poverty.

He asked his brothers to remove his tunic and lay him naked on the ground. There he lay with his left hand covering the wound in his side. Seeing him thus lie, the Father Guardian of the Portiuncula brought his own tunic and breeches to cover him, and to forestall Francis' refusal he said to him, "I lend you this tunic and breeches, and in order that you may know you have no right of property in them, I deprive you of all power to give them to anyone else." Francis' face lit up with joy, and for two reasons, for this speech was meant as acknowledgment that Francis had always been true to his vows of poverty, but it was tender and teasing also, a remembrance of the many times that Francis, to the despair of the brothers, had given away all that he possessed.

When they put him back on his bed, he was content though in much pain. The next morning he asked for his brothers, and for a loaf of bread to be broken in pieces, and he gave to each of them. This was their last meal together.

When he was about to die, he asked again to be laid on the ground, and with what voice was left to him, he sang the 142nd Psalm, beginning, "I cried unto the Lord with my voice; with my voice unto the Lord did I make my supplication," and ending, "Bring my soul out of prison, that I may praise thy name; the righteous shall compass me about, for thou shalt deal bountifully with me."

And having so sung, he died.

ELIZABETH GOUDGE'S SAINT FRANCIS OF ASSISI

Some people say that the days of faith are over, that Francis of Assisi lived in times that will never be known again, and that is why he was able to die singing. Such people should read that glorious book *Dying We Live*, which contains the last letters of German men and women, some of them very young, who accepted death under Hitler rather than, as Mr. George N. Shuster states, "lose their integrity." What do those words mean: "lose their integrity"? Mr. Shuster seems to suggest that it is something one keeps even though one is dead. And this is a proper thought about a book called by the title *Dying We Live*.

This book is so full of courage, faith, and compassion for those who will be bereaved, and gratitude and surprise that God should have selected such weak instruments, that one could quote it for ever. I shall quote only one thing. On February 18, 1943, Hans Scholl (23) and his sister Susie (21) were caught dropping copies of the leaflet *Pamphlet of the White Rose* from a gallery into the main

120

lobby of the University of Munich. One wonders at such courage in 1943, at the time when the Russians were turning the tide of war. One of this group was Christoph Probst (23). He was sentenced to death on February 21, and executed on February 22. His mother and sister were allowed to read his farewell letters in the presence of the Gestapo, but were not allowed to keep them. This is how they remembered them:

To his mother: I thank you for having given me life. When I really think it through, it has all been a single road to God. Do not grieve that I must now skip the last part of it. Soon I shall be closer to you than before. In the meantime I'll prepare a glorious reception for you all.

To his sister: I never knew dying is so easy. . . . I die without any feeling of hatred. . . . Never forget that life is nothing but a growing in love and a preparation for eternity.

O my most blessed and glorious Creator, thou hast fed me all my life long, and redeemed me from all evil: seeing it is Thy merciful pleasure to take me out of this frail body, and to wipe away all tears from mine eyes, and all sorrows from my heart, I do with all humility and willingness consent and submit myself wholly unto Thy sacred will. My most loving Redeemer, into Thy saving and everlasting arms I commend my spirit: I am ready, my dear Lord, and earnestly expect and long for Thy good pleasure. Come quickly, and receive the soul of Thy servant which trusteth in Thee. HENRY VAUGHAN

Lord, give me grace to die in Thy will. Prepare me for whatever place or condition awaits me. Let me die true to those things I believe to be true. And suffer me not through any fear of death to fall from Thee.

Lord, give me grace to live in Thy will also. Help me to master any fear, any desire, that prevents me from living in Thy will. Make me, O Lord, the instrument of Thy peace, that I may know eternal life.

Into Thy hands I commend my spirit.

21

However that may be, each one must order his life according to the gift the Lord has granted him and his condition when God called him. That is what I teach in all our congregations. Was a man called with the marks of circumcision on him? Let him not remove them. Was he uncircumcised when he was called? Let him not be circumcised. Circumcision or uncircumcision is neither here nor there; what matters is to keep God's commands. Every man should remain in the condition in which he was called. Were you a slave when you were called? Do not let that trouble you; but if a chance of liberty should come, take it. For the man who as a slave received the call to be a Christian is the Lord's freedman, and, equally, the free man who received the call is a slave in the service of Christ.

You were bought at a price; do not become the slaves of men.   PAUL TO THE CORINTHIANS
(1 COR: 7:17–23 NEB)

When St. Paul writes of slavery and freedom, he is writing of institutions of his own times. But he is also playing on the words, and what he has to say has a meaning not dependent on time or place. He is saying that the man who is a slave of Christ is free, and that the man who is free in Christ is a slave.

It is hard to comprehend this twofold paradox, yet we often comprehend it readily enough in other spheres. When we hear great music, we say that we are spellbound. When we hear great speaking, we say that the speaker holds us; perhaps we add, in the hollow of his hand. A great actress enthrals us, literally holds us in thrall. A book grips us. A song captivates us. I think it was the Americans who introduced to the English language the expression "I am sold" (presumably into some kind of captivity).

One common element in all these bondages is the experience of being free. It is in being bound that we are free; not only free, but in some exciting way free.

Another common element is the element of love. We say we love music, if it binds us and makes us free. We say we love the theatre, if it enthrals us and makes us free. We say we love a game, if it fascinates us and makes us free. The music, the play, the book, may make us weep, may fill us with that indescribable mixture of pain and joy, but what makes us weep and dance and laugh is not just the music or the play or the book, it is something that rises in us: we are glad to be what we are; we have been caught up into that bondage which is perfect freedom.

When I was a young man, my student days over, I was influenced for a while by an unwilling belief in a rigid determinism, that choice and will were illusory, that we are what we are because of all the external forces that made us: our parents, friends, school, society, world, our physiology and our metabolism, and all the rest of them.

I lived in a race-caste·society, and I was determined to get out of it, although it was physically more comfortable to live in it, to identify with it, even to be ready to die for it. What force was working there inside me? Was it simply another product of parents, friends, school, society, world, physiology, metabolism? Yes, in a way it was. But today I believe that was nothing more than an out-view, one which saw myself as a tool, a toy, a thing to be moved about by forces external to myself. Today I do not underestimate these external forces; today I hold an in-view, one which sees myself as a self, made no doubt by many forces beyond my control, but gaining in coherence and integrity as I grow older. I am no longer a determinist; I am, in so far as a man can be, a self-determinator. That is one of the freedoms that the gospel gives to us, a belief in our worth as persons, a belief in what we can *do* as persons, a belief in what we can *be*. And no one helped me more to understand it than Francis of Assisi.

Why did Jesus hold spellbound those who listened to him? It was because he showed them they were not helpless victims in the grip of fears, hates, the past, the world. They were the salt of the earth, the light of the world. He showed them a new thing—that obedience and freedom are inseparable. For where is the joy of living in a society in which all obey and none is free? Or in which all are free and none obeys? Something in them rose up to meet him; they were caught up into the bondage which is the perfect freedom; they became his servants and his freedmen; they became his followers and his disciples; in him they found meaning for their lives, and there is no freedom like the freedom of finding meaning for one's life, of becoming the instrument of a Lord who helps us to be what we were meant to be. Yet many resist him, believing that to follow him is to lose the whole world.

It was granted to a sinner, not to a saint, to say this in unforgettable words—Francis Thompson in "The Hound of Heaven."

I fled Him, down the nights and down the days;
    I fled Him, down the arches of the years;
I fled Him, down the labyrinthine ways
    Of my own mind; and in the mist of tears
I hid from Him, and under running laughter.
        Up vistaed hopes I sped;
        And shot, precipitated,
Adown titanic glooms of chasmèd fears,
    From those strong Feet that followed, followed after.
        But with unhurrying chase,
        And unperturbèd pace,
Deliberate speed, majestic instancy,
        They beat—and a Voice beat
        More instant than the Feet—
"All things betray thee, who betrayest Me."

        I pleaded, outlaw-wise,
By many a hearted casement, curtained red,
    Trellised with intertwining charities;
(For though I knew His love who followèd,
        Yet was I sore adread
Lest, having Him, I must have naught beside.)
But, if one little casement parted wide,
    The gust of His approach would clash it to,
    Fear wist not to evade, as Love wist to pursue.

And that is the heart of it—"yet was I sore adread, lest, having Him, I must have naught beside." The dread of St. Augustine also—"give me chastity and continency, but do not give it yet." The dread that was overcome by the grace of God when Francis of Assisi came down from his horse and kissed the leper on the Umbrian plain.

THE PRISON HOUSE

I ran from the prison house but they captured me,
And he waited me at the door with a face of doom,
And motioned me to go to his private room,
And he took my rank from me and gave me the hell
Of his tongue, and ordered me to the runaway cell
With the walls and the chains and the long night-days and
    the gloom.

And once on leave that goes to the well-behaved
I rose in fright from the very brothel bed
And through the midnight streets like a mad thing fled
Sobbing with fear lest the door be closed on me,
But nothing he did to me, he let me be,
No word but your clothing's disarranged he said.

And once in a place where I was, a man did ask
Whence I was, and he said, I never thought to see
A man from that place, and I wish I could be
In that place, by God I wish that I could be there,
I wish I was there, and I went back on air
And he met me there at the door, and he smiled at me.

And once when he took the whip to my rebel flesh
With foul and magnificent words I cursed and reviled

His name and his house and his works, and drunken and
 wild
I took the whip from his hands and slashed him again
And again and again, so he paid the price for my pain,
Till I fell at his feet and wept on the stone like a child.

He can take the hide from my back, and the sight from
 my eyes,
The lust of my loins, and the comforts of memory,
Fruit's taste, and the scent of the flowers, the salt of the
 sea,
The sounds of the world, and the words of magic and fire
That comforted me, so long as he does not require
The chains that now are become like garments to me.

   Lord, we give thanks for the life and works of Thy
servant and freedman Francis of Assisi, and for the help
and hope that knowledge of his life has given to us and to
countless others.
   Lord, make us also the instruments of Thy peace.